What people say about this book

Den er meget fængende, sjov og man har lyst til at læse videre!
My Mum
*(a rough translation from Danish: It's very catchy
and funny and you want to keep reading!)*

I can totally relate to putting myself first, loving myself more, not fixing things for others. This is a topic that a lot of women can relate to in today's world. We women are excellent multitaskers, juggling so much. It's important we find a way to delegate, juggle less to allow more time for ourselves, love ourselves more and put ourselves first.
Clarissa High, Owner Natural Fall Hair Design, mother of 2 plus 2 dogs

As always very insightful, and a lot of food for thought!
Very good inspiration and hacks to the very important
everyday life, especially if you got a little lost.
*Charlotte N. Frandsen, Leverage Finance Professional,
mother of 1 daughter and 1 Golden Retriever*

All wannabe superwomen can get a wake-up call and a kind and loving kick as Annlone shares her relatable everyday stories in an unapologetic no-nonsense voice. The bite-size chunks are easily read for you to reflect on.
Jane Balle, Founder Mindful Making, mother of 3

It's a pleasure to read this book. I love how the message
in each story or narrative has the potential to linger either
because it brought you pleasure, laughter, a walk down
memory lane or something to take with you today or tomorrow.
*Brenda Stewart, mother of 2 and part of
Goodbye Superwoman's original group workshops*

I think any over-achiever can relate.
Anja Poehlmann, National Finance and Commercial Lead, mother of 2

Many of us need to be perfectionists at work and it's important to
allow ourselves time, remembering it might be okay or even advisable
to tone down that quality when not at work. To have patience.
This book gives refreshing tips on how to start this important work.
Britt Lange, Senior Anaesthesiologist, PhD, MBA, mother of 3

Wow! Goodbye Superwoman struck such a chord, multiple times in so
many ways. So many of us need to leave behind all the striving, the being
more, the endless comparison, never being enough and instead sign up
for the adventure of BEING MORE ME. The opportunity for reflections,
the lightness, the generous perspective, and the well curated journey:
I highly recommend you go on this journey with Adventurer Annlone.
*Julie Johnson, Agrileadership Founder,
1 treasured husband, 3 kids, 3 horses and 1 devoted dog*

52 Sunday blogs to help us realise how over-achieving is not the way forward

ANNLONE DALHOFF

First published 2023 by Annlone Dalhoff

Produced by Independent Ink
independentink.com.au

Copyright © Annlone Dalhoff 2023

The moral right of the author to be identified as the author of this work has been asserted.

All rights reserved. Except as permitted under the *Australian Copyright Act 1968*, no part of this publication may be reproduced, stored in a retrieval system, or transmitted in any form or by any means, electronic, mechanical, photocopying, recording or otherwise, without prior written permission from the publisher. All enquiries should be made to the author.

Cover design by Catucci Design
Edited by Daina Lindeman
Typeset by Post Pre-press Group, Brisbane

ISBN 978-0-6459766-0-1 (paperback)
ISBN 978-0-6459766-1-8 (epub)
ISBN 978-0-6459766-2-5 (kindle)

Disclaimer:
Any information in the book is purely the opinion of the author based on personal experience and should not be taken as business or legal advice. All material is provided for educational purposes only. We recommend to always seek the advice of a qualified professional before making any decision regarding personal and business needs.

For our daughters

tak, tak, tak

52 Sunday Blogs
(well, 53 to be correct)

The cost of being Superwoman
1	Superwoman down with man flu!	2
2	Have you ever seen a perfectionist having fun? Like real fun?	6
3	"Step away …" I said, "Step away!"	10
4	Working mums – why does that combination of words even exist?	14
5	Goodbye, Superwoman!	18

Foundational life hacks
6	My daily joy levels … are up to ME??!!	24
7	A passion? No, I don't have time for that …	28
8	A hobby?? Isn't that for retired people?	32
9	How to find six hours a week – for YOU.	36
10	Outsource!! No, you didn't pick up a business magazine – this is for you.	42
11	Sitting still for an hour – just one!	46
12	Being crazy – the fun way!	50

Creating our ideal average day

13 Jeg holder af hverdagen. 56
14 What makes your heart sing? 60
15 What's worse: lying to others or to yourself? 64
16 Time management to perfection – including time to relax! 68
17 That awesome fifth day?! 72
18 Just stay home one weekend – just one. 78
19 Washing clothes – is it that time of year again? 82
20 What I really want for Christmas … 86

Shifting our language and mindset

21 All emotions welcome … oh, noooooo!! 92
22 "Don't think of a pink elephant." I said, "DON'T think of a pink elephant." 96
23 The little BUT … 100
24 Me … butthurt?! The four steps to owning your own stuff. 104

Fear and risky vs safe problems

25 Honey, the kids have shrunk! 112
26 'Cuse me – is that lipstick on your teeth??! 116
27 Can this be returned? Please. 120
28 One foot on the brake. 124

Generosity and empowerment

29 Are you a giver or a getter??   130
30 OMG – am I an introvert??   134
31 Living selfishly (yes, that's OK!).   138

It's all a strategy

32 How do you brush your teeth?   144
33 Sushi train of thoughts.   150
34 Asking myself what??   154

Bringing structure to our life

35 I love my morning jog. You what??   160
36 Who says carrots are not a meal??   164
37 Letting go – or go away for a week or two.   170

Wealth buckets and I-am-ness

38 A trusting matter?   176
39 You can't afford it? Well, well … how much STUFF do you buy??   180
40 You are so beautiful … Who me??!   184
41 Saying NO. Plainly NO.   188

From ambition-driven to meaning-driven

42 I want it NOW! 196
43 Follow yourself. 200
44 When a lot is not enough … 204
45 Two years from now – who are you? 210
46 Like teenagers again. 214

Deepen your connections

47 No pets allowed – well, maybe a bunny if you force me. 220
48 Nature? No, thanks. I tend to kill any plants within a 20-metre radius. 224
49 Young girls out there – listen to that inner voice! 228
50 Meditation – HA! I bet my brain will never be able to stop racing. 232

Say yes and work out how

51 Me – masculine??!!! That wasn't the goal … 238
52 One year for women – or one day? 244
53 Keep turning up! 248

Yes, to tease the perfectionist in you (that I know way too well) 53 blogs made the cut, not 52 as announced. Just like every fourth year we have an extra day inserted in February to fit it all in, I thought I would give you an extra blog. Complimentary. A gift from me to you. And mainly because I had done the hard cut halving the blogs and simply couldn't cut any further. There you go. Enjoy!

Introduction

I wasn't told lies. I had all the opportunities in the world and walked straight into the trouble myself. Of wanting to be and do it all. Being Superwoman: driving my career, having a family, continuing my hobbies, looking after my health, and being a good mum, daughter, friend, wife, leader, colleague, and neighbour all at the same time. Wanting to look good and be liked by all, while getting my voice heard and pushing the worthy agendas. Definitely no time for the news or TV.

Growing up in Denmark in a loving, supportive family, I was allowed and encouraged to be ME. I didn't view life through labels, didn't think about the limitations of being a girl or the shortest person around. I just went for the first row and never looked back.

Not everyone, or maybe very few, are lucky to grow up like I did.

But no matter the story, way too many of us try too hard to be more, to be something other than what we are. We endlessly compare and strive.

With this book, I hope to start a revolution of being ourselves. Not trying to be it all. Not trying to be like the rigid role models around us. There is only ONE you. Make the most of it.

To do that, we have to say goodbye and let go of many things — perfectionism, worrying about what others think about us, being afraid of being weak, just to name a few. I've been brave and have said goodbye. And therefore hello.

Hello to being me while caring about others and the greater good. It starts with daring to first put on your own oxygen mask. Asking yourself what you really want. And then being brave enough to follow that direction, bit by bit, despite what those around you may say, feel or think about that path.

Welcome to my journey. I hope my stories, my Sunday blogs, will inspire you to be more you. To find out what your ideal life looks like. Not just keep running and running trying to catch up to an ideal that may not even suit you.

Gute Reise as they say in Germany. God tur as they say in Denmark. Or 'Go for it mate' as we say in Australia.

Practical Notes

★ My journey and the "kicks and carrots" in these blogs are probably most relevant for working women with kids. The marketing professional in me would add "aged 25–65". But finding and then following ourselves may be relevant to you, too, no matter your age, gender or circumstances. Feel welcomed and invited to read on. And if you chose the e-version, feel free to also buy a physical copy for your bookshelf. You never know when a neighbour, friend, kid's friend or colleague will happen to notice it and borrow it, because that's exactly what they needed that day. Let's pay it forward. It's never too early or too late. The right time is now.

- ★ It's Sunday blogs for a reason. Reading one a week and gradually shifting your perspective creates a big impact twelve months down the track. The blogs were originally posted on Sundays for the over-achievers to get bite-sized tricks before passing out as another week was about to start.

- ★ The blogs in this book are sorted to give you a journey from 1 to 53, following the journey of awareness and learning I went through. This collection is chosen from hundreds of weekly blogs I wrote and shared on social media and in newsletters over eight years through my Joy Hearts coaching business. But feel free to use the random pick method to choose a blog number every Sunday night (or whenever you read or listen to my voice). That's how I enjoyed reading Don't Sweat the Small Stuff (and it's all small stuff), which you must read if you haven't.

- ★ For the detail-oriented amongst you, keep breathing as you read through the blogs and notice the age of me and our daughters doing weird jumps. The chosen blogs represent insights from nearly a decade. Same me. Same husband. Same kids. Just different phases of our lives. Anyway, I'll let you get started.

The cost of being Superwoman

For you, your kids, your partner and yourself

Superwoman down with man flu!

When Superwomen are sick, we just keep going. Power through. Work. Do all the things that have to be done.

I'm working on getting rid of Superwoman. And a good opportunity arose this week, when I realised I had powered through because of lots of VERY important things. Trying to hide the fact that I was sick by changing plans (working from home midweek) but still getting all the same things done, keeping to all the same deadlines. THIS HAS TO STOP!

Who was I kidding? Myself. Looking after everybody else's needs when my body was clearly telling me, "ENOUGH!"

So, after a night of coughing, I realised men do it right. They get the man flu. They're sick. They're OUT. Decision made right there and then. They declare man flu and pull the plug. Cancel everything for the next 48 hours. Do you know how hard that is? Instead, you keep coming up with excuses of why you could still do x and join y, even if just with a phone call. Full stop. NO!

You will hear me teaching you how to say NO later on, in Blog 41. It takes training, as you'll learn, and sometimes even a stomp of the foot! It's not easy, and I have to remind myself to take my own advice and my own medicine (pun intended) all the time.

One of our daughters went downhill with a virus, and cleverly cancelled everything straight away when she felt it coming on. She got so much better during the week because she rested and was ready for everything planned for later. The other one powered through, like me (role modelling ... argh ... ??!!), and to no one's surprise, she only got worse as the week progressed.

That night, in those early morning hours of coughing, I told my inner Superwoman to take a break. Actually, to pack her suitcase (does she even have one?) and just go. Leave. To never come back.

And I'm honouring myself, not everyone else or my packed calendar. Superwoman has left the building. Man flu has inspired me. I'm off sick. I'm out. I'm done.

The real wake-up call, in those early hours, was remembering it was only three months ago I was tumbling down the same rabbit hole. And ended up with no voice for more than a month. At least this time, I realised I was on the way down the same rabbit hole, and that I needed to find a way out soon.

Next time, I'll see it coming, stay clear, and save myself all the drama of extended suffering. I'll walk down a totally different path.

Goodbye, Superwoman. Welcome home, Me.

Which rabbit hole will you practise getting out of?

★ **Reflections?**

> PAUSE and take a minute to notice what came up for you. You'll be surprised how our brain and body come up with random ideas when we let them. Capture your thoughts with some doodles, drawings or bullet points. I tell you, it works!

★ **One action I'll take**

Have you ever seen a perfectionist having fun? Like real fun?

When did you last have a real belly laugh? Not a *tee-hee* or *haha*, but one that builds up and explodes, that shakes your whole body? I bet it didn't happen while you were washing up. Or ironing. Or doing the kids' lunches. Or stressing over all the work and emails you need to get done tonight/later/this weekend. If a laugh escaped you then, it would have been a nervous ha-ha-ha, jaws tight, stiff fake smile.

Are you taking yourself (and everyone else) too seriously? When was the last time you just threw out a loud laugh when your kids or anyone else asked you to do something?

It's good to be serious about what you do. Both at home and at work. It's great to be ambitious. It works even better if it flows naturally, if you are fully present and engaged and energised while perfecting something. But if your mind is going crazy with things you should/could/must do or just worries, you are perfecting nothing. You are stressing yourself – and everyone else – out!

Time for a confession. I was SO perfectionistic. SO serious. Before we got married and were living together, I was SO embarrassed when my then-boyfriend was goofing around (even if it was just the two of us in the apartment), putting silly things on his head and playing the clown. My toes curled and nearly crumbled.

Now see me, nearly 20 years wiser. Appreciating his humour and goofing around – I even allow some great belly laughs to escape me! Thank you! For being persistent. For continuing to NOT take yourself or me so seriously.

So the answer is no. I was not having real fun while being a perfectionist. All I could manage were a few polite or reflex *hahas* that didn't connect to anything below the throat level. I practised and learned to let go – it makes things so much easier. I know you can as well. Just once a week to get started, find a situation you normally stress about and let go.

Happy laughing and goofing around!

★ **Reflections?**

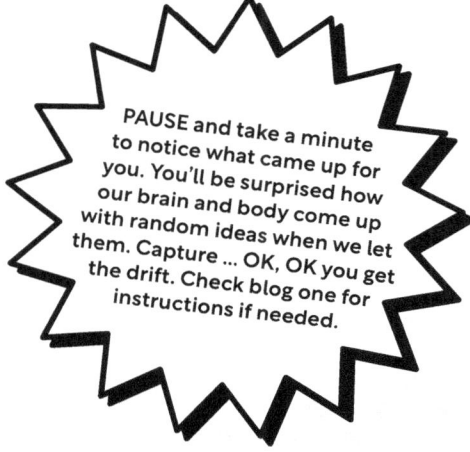

PAUSE and take a minute to notice what came up for you. You'll be surprised how our brain and body come up with random ideas when we let them. Capture ... OK, OK you get the drift. Check blog one for instructions if needed.

★ **One action I'll take**

"Step away …"
I say, "Step away!"

How come we believe we know best? That things will be quicker/better/more efficient if WE do it all? "Step away …" I say, "Step away!"

Picture this. An airport. Smart gates. A mother (with the best of intentions for the kids, herself, and the greater good) pushing one passport at a time through the slot, ushering one kid through at a time, as though she is running a military operation. I don't notice if she also does it for her husband, which still bugs me …

That's over-functioning. We all do it. Take away the opportunity for someone else to do it THEIR way. It may have been the BEST part of the trip for those kids, sliding the passport into the machine themselves, stepping onto the feet marks on the floor. Not rocket science. No commands needed. She takes away a chance for empowerment, really. They will figure it out by watching the ones in front of them in the queue. Like they learn everything else. Not from what others say, but what people around them DO.

So where are YOU over-functioning? With staff, kids, partners, parents, friends, pets, gardening, housework … Which commands and controls are worthy of retirement?

"Step away …" I say, "Step away!"

⭐ Reflections?

I know you would be really annoyed (and it would work against the message in this blog) if we included the instructions again, so all good, you know the drill!

⭐ One action I'll take

Working mums — why does that combination of words even exist?

Growing up in Denmark, I was very fortunate to never think of myself as a girl as such, or about what girls could or should do. Denmark is so egalitarian (when seen from the other side of the globe). Both men and women drop off and pick up kids. Both men and women work, cook, do the washing, become prime ministers or nurses. And kids grow up as kids, not as "girls" or "boys".

It has gone so far that I started feeling sorry for the Danish men, having no turf left to just be men, having become so understanding of women's needs and thoughts, not taking space to be REAL men (what is that anyway?). But at the same time, I admire them greatly; within generations, they have morphed into a new species of understanding humans — not just capable of understanding women but of understanding life, themselves, and what's important.

Because of this background, I felt SO offended when I moved to Australia and heard combinations of words I would have been happy to never learn: class mum, working mum, soccer mum …

And I nearly complained to the headmaster when on Mother's Day I got a thank you card from my daughter that she had made at school. She had added the drawings, but the pre-printed message said: "Thank you for the cooking. Thank you for the lunch boxes. Thank you for the mending …" I burst into hysterical laughter, not believing my own eyes. I explained to my daughter that I was so happy about the drawings, and that I hope to be SO much more to my children, myself, my husband, and the world than a "supplier of services". I felt like I had been transported back five decades.

I never thought about being a female leader – until I hit the ground in Australia. I never thought of having fewer opportunities or dreams for the future than any of my male friends. And in Denmark, we only know of co-ed schools. Life is kind of co-ed, isn't it?

So dear daughters, dear men, dear women. Please see all the people around you as just that. People. Humans. Individuals. Each with a unique personality. And quirks and talents. There's no need to put us into boxes. It's great to have role models and people you connect with – but don't pre-empt and cut off half the opportunities you have for great relationships, at work or elsewhere. And don't cut off half of your inner abilities.

Well, that wasn't a funny blog as usual, but I needed to get it out.

Thank you for being YOU.

★ Reflections?

Pssst ... we're not putting anyone in a box. Go back to blog 1 for the instruction blurb.

★ One action I'll take

Goodbye, Superwoman!

Are you a fixer? Constantly working hard to fix the world and those around you? Aha!! We may just have spotted another Superwoman in action.

This week, we ran a workshop where saying goodbye to Superwoman resonated. So many successful, talented, good-hearted women work so hard both at home and at work, keeping the wheels turning and fixing it all. Especially, fixing those around them.

What if your true success doesn't come from fixing? What if, instead, it's letting go of the idea that you can fix everything and have an answer for it all?

You may have heard rumours about women who are not really PART of their families, who are not sitting down having a great laugh with them, who are not enjoying being present. I'm SURE you are not one of them, but you may have heard of someone like that??!! Well, I know one. It was me for decades. And she still pops by on occasions – because she's so familiar and gets shit done.

What if you practised saying goodbye to her? Goodbye to the idea that you are the one with the answer, the one with the right schedule for "how life should be lived around here". And instead, you started BEING. What if there was much less doing, and much more being?

It may just happen that you join in on a joke because you are actually listening enough to hear it. That you have a laugh because you are actually present and not in your head, planning the next thing to get done …

Ouch … I know a lot of you recognise this. Are you up for the challenge? To take the journey of finding out what true happiness could look like. What the meaning of true success is for you. What loving and living truly could feel like. To start becoming the person you really would love to spend time with – not the commander-in-chief keeping all at a safe distance through being busy.

Not fixing the world and those around us. But accepting that we are FULL of contrasts, accepting all of us, and starting to become truly powerful?

Goodbye, Superwoman. Hello, real you.

I hope you're ready to make a change. To not finish next year feeling the same way as you do now (or worse). But twelve months from now feeling different and already seeing changes around you. It doesn't happen overnight, it happens day by day through intention and tiny changes. I would love to have you join the movement. Let's make it a global one: of less doing and more being!

★ **Reflections?**

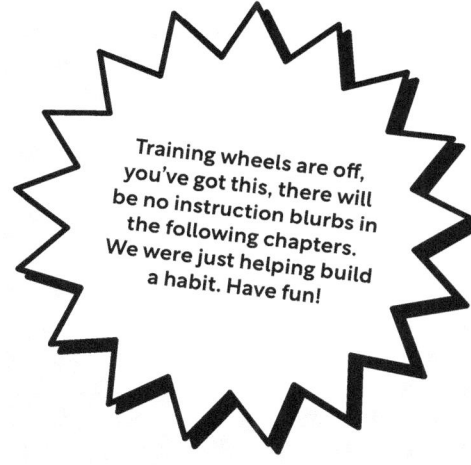

Training wheels are off, you've got this, there will be no instruction blurbs in the following chapters. We were just helping build a habit. Have fun!

★ **One action I'll take**

Foundational life hacks

Why didn't we all learn this stuff in school?

My daily joy levels ... are up to ME??!!

Most of our self-talk is about how our kids, partner, neighbours, boss, colleagues, parents, dog … (please continue the list yourself) … are the reason for our bad mood right now. Here's some news: your daily joy levels are up to YOU.

 AUTHOR'S NOTE: If you're in a state of depression, this is not for you. You need to ask for help. As you, with help, work your way out of the fog, you will get tools that help you realise what helps and hinders your thoughts and moods. See one example in blog 33. Don't blame yourself, ask for help. Sending you lots of love.

Yes, circumstances and emotions and buttons being pushed impact us. I get it. I let them impact me all the time. I've coached and witnessed rainy days and days that turn into constant grey (no, I'm not talking about the Danish weather). The liberation comes when you realise it IS up to you, that no matter how frustrating or annoying (pick your favourite "what-ruins-it-for-me-word") the situation or person is, it is how you REACT that matters. To how you feel. To how you trust yourself.

So, take a step back. Go for a walk. Have a cup of tea. Start realising WHO you really want to be. How that ideal you will react to the situation (in a million years, when you have practised enough ...). That's when life starts giving you energy instead of draining you. When you can take every encounter or challenge as another opportunity for practising who you are becoming. And guess what? As you start, you realise it won't take a million years. That you actually ARE changing bit by bit every time you react (or wisely choose not to react!) as the human being you are becoming.

Have a play with it. Try it on for a week. Look at all the things that "happen to you" as what they are — external events. And recognise that you, by your response, have a massive effect on the outcome.

Thank yourself for having a go. And ask for help if this is a big one. Which joy levels are you aiming for in the next 24 hours? Go, you!

★ **Reflections?**

★ **One action I'll take**

A passion? No, I don't have time for that ...

Follow your passion! Why? Hmm … let me see: it would make you happy, fill your days and weeks with joy, give you energy for all the other things in life. Is that reason enough?

I'm really good at following my passions. Some may say I'm selfish — or could you perhaps say I'm focused? Housework is overrated. It will always come back, take all of your "spare time", and possibly deplete any humour reserves you had left, so why not leave it for now and read a good book instead?

I have many passions. That's a safe way of always having an outlet that fits your mood, the weather, and how much time you have up your sleeve. Singing with others is one, painting random abstract pictures, reading, writing, running through the bush, just sitting and thinking. How good is that for variety?

Oh, did I mention "having time"? You are never given time. You have to TAKE time to do the things you love, and put them up the top of your list (yes, I also make to-do lists!) because NOW is the best time to do them. I proudly tell colleagues and friends how I can sit in the middle of a room where it looks like a bomb has gone off — and read. After having done what I love, I have so much more energy and will get the rest of the things on my list done much more easily (and without wanting to kill anyone), so it's even safer for both my family and myself! How's that for a win-win?

Anyway, what's YOUR passion? What makes you happy, makes you forget time? If the answer doesn't pop up easily, leave the question to simmer, and I'll be back next week. Because now I'm off on a walk, in my precious 20 minutes before attacking today's list. See you!

★ **Reflections?**

★ **One action I'll take**

A hobby?? Isn't that for retired people?

OK, here's a secret: I'm 44 and have already spent SO many hours of my life doing things I love. If you start counting, how many hours did you spend this week on YOU and something you really like doing? If you can count them on one hand, GET MOVING on putting yourself and your passions up the top of the list. (How did I know you have a to-do list? Well, don't we all?)

I love singing. I always have. From when I was a kid, in choirs, bands, musicals – you name it. Most women stop celebrating their birthdays at some point, and in general, stop celebrating anything remotely fun in their lives – especially when the kids come along. But that's insane. You need to celebrate more than ever from then on! So I kept singing. It isn't always easy, and sometimes I drag myself to choir on a Thursday night. But guess what? I always leave with steps that are lighter and a smile on my face.

So singing is my "breathing space". When we had our first child, only two weeks passed before I was out the door to sing (breathe!). And when we moved to the other side of the world for my job, it took half a year before I came to my senses and realised I was in deep despair, stress, and denial – I needed to find some people to sing (breathe!) with.

You make others happier if you start off in a state of being happy yourself. Selfish? Yes. To be sure to be the best YOU that you can be. And then have bucketloads of energy to give.

What's YOUR passion? What makes you smile and feel good? How can you carve out six hours of that, just for you? You don't have time? Get up earlier, start buying clothes that don't need ironing ... Do you know what? Let's talk next time about the thousand things in everyday life we could spend less time on. Enjoy unravelling what your passion is until then!

★ **Reflections?**

★ **One action I'll take**

How to find six hours a week – for YOU.

In the previous blog, I talked about how important it is to find things that you are passionate about. That make you smile and feel good. That make you feel alive. And how you will not be given time for your passions. You need to TAKE the time. And I'm not talking about just a few minutes — six hours is more like it! I can already hear you saying that you don't know how you can possibly find the time. Well, here's how.

'Eat more carrots.' 'Do more exercise.' 'You need 8 hours of sleep.' This is my advice to you: stop reading gossip and women's magazines and scrolling social media feeds. Just trust your own instincts and common sense. Da-daaaa — I just gave you back one hour a week.

 AUTHOR'S NOTE: As this was written ten years ago, your viewing time is probably several hours a day by now, not just an hour a week. See it as a bonus: more time to take back.

Stop ironing. I'm not kidding. Just stop. Buy clothes that don't need it. Dry your washing on hangers — and then put it straight into the cupboard. If you or your partner need business shirts for work — pay a dry-cleaning service to clean and iron them. Or make a plan to change jobs (or the dress code at work. It may take a bit of effort, but trust me, it's possible. And you will all feel better and more yourselves). How many hours did you get into your "hours for just ME" bank? Honestly? OK, two hours.

Make the kids do their own lunchboxes. OK, skip this if you have toddlers. But for the rest of you, ask your kids to be part of the tribe — show them you NEED them to keep the "family farm" running. No "stars" or pocket money; they just need to do stuff. That's two hours at least. See the first week as an investment from your side and act as an advisor. But kids are clever and actually end up liking being useful.

Shopping. For hours. Including chatting to the whole neighbourhood and ending up in three more shops than planned. Be focused, head to the planned shop, buy what you have on the shopping list (YES, only those things), head straight home, and get the family to unpack. Stay focused, three hours saved.

 AUTHOR'S NOTE: If we learnt to do one thing during the pandemic, it was to shop online. This can save you hours, but it can become a black hole, too! Stay focused

---

Don't watch TV. NO TV. You may seem boring at work when you can't talk about the latest *Masterchef* or *Dancing with the Stars*. But did any of these programs ever make you feel really happy and super energised to get up and do things yourself? Five hours right there for YOU.

We already have thirteen hours — and haven't even started running out of ideas! Have fun continuing the list yourself! I'm off to put on some funky music and have a little crazy dance around the living room. See you!

★ **Reflections?**

★ **One action I'll take**

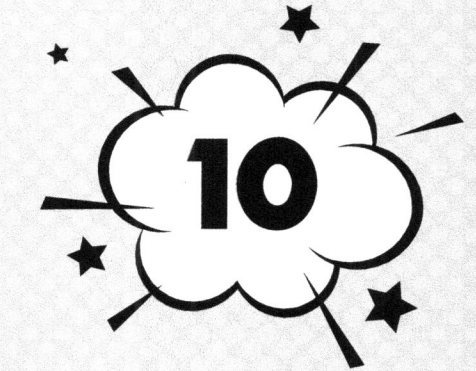

Outsource!! No, you didn't pick up a business magazine — this is for you.

Here's a funny one for a rainy afternoon. Mentally hire a consulting group. Imagine them walking in your front door (these guys never come through the back door), black suits and all, half your age, and very serious. Embrace them. They'll refuse the cup of tea you offer – their eyes are already set on the target. Let them be.

Now imagine them analysing, bit by bit, your whole life (incredibly scary, I know!!). Every action you take from when you get out of bed on a Monday morning till when you collapse on the same bed Sunday night, not knowing how another week passed by.

They will check which things you are GREAT at doing yourself – and which tasks you should delegate (oh, I can feel your nervous tics starting; the panic of letting go is moving through your body!!). You will start explaining why ONLY you can do this and that, but these guys don't care – it's all excuses!

Whisper to me the first thing that comes to mind that you are NOT good at and would love to let go of (be honest here!): cleaning, doing your taxes, baking that birthday cake, planning the next event at your club, making that dreaded call to the bank to complain? (All of the above??)

Mediocre doesn't make anyone happy, so the action plan they will present to you is as follows: focus on things you are GREAT at, practise the things you are reasonable at, and let go of the hate list items. Negotiate with your partner/kids/girlfriend and get them to do those things. Ask for favours, and return the favours with stuff you are great at. Or pay people who are better than you to do those particular things. You can't afford it? Let's talk another time about the endless stuff you spend money on that you don't need!

My #1 is cleaning. Paying someone fortnightly – and coming home to a fresh, clean house – is just the best. No arguing or bad conscience all weekend. We have paid for this since we were young. Doesn't matter what your mum/neighbours/others say!!! It's about YOU. We would rather let go of our second car than let go of our cleaner.

So what #1 hate item will you outsource? Do I really need to send in those guys, or are you ready to whisper it out loud? Change it before the end of the month. GO!!

★ **Reflections?**

★ **One action I'll take**

Sitting still for an hour – just one!

Here's a test for you. Not like the women's magazine ones that tell you if you're a dreamer or a doer. A real hands-on one, or actually more of a bums-on one. Sit still for an hour at home. Yep, for 60 full minutes.

Your brain will start a to-do list within seconds (should do the washing, have to call Sue). Just ignore it. Then your body will feel itchy. You see a sock under the couch with a month's worth of dust attached to it that you NEED to retrieve. Don't. Then your bad conscience is back: *I can't just sit here.* Yes, you can. Just tell it right back: *Yes, I can!*

OK, you managed 2 minutes and 10 seconds. Well done! Celebrate your successes! Now is the time to do something you like. Grab a book, a writing pad (NOT for to-do lists; only for writing things like a diary, 10 things you're grateful for, a poem that doesn't rhyme, drawing doodles), your knitting, or anything remotely recreational.

Now comes the real test: your children/partner/mum/neighbour walks in. Keep seated. Look even more concentrated at your doodles. Pretend you haven't seen them. (Oooh, how can that feel SO difficult? Where does that pleasing gene actually sit?)

And now you'll experience the most fun you've probably had all week (because most women officially stop having fun just after getting married/having children/you fill it in). They will ask in wonder:

"What are you doing???" Don't take it as an insult. They have just never seen you sitting still, in your home, doing "nothing". Ever.

And then you calmly reply: "I just felt like reading a book/knitting, etc." Don't explain. Say no more. Just concentrate back on the doodles. They will think you have gone mad, and how much fun is that, surprising both them and yourself? If they scale up the pressure ("When are we having dinner?"/"Where is my …?"), you calmly respond: "I don't know. I'm just having an hour for myself."

Easy? No. Maybe practise on your own first without the optional escalation. Aaaaaah, letting go of that perfectionism, the duties … aaaaah. Well done. Lesson one complete!

★ **Reflections?**

★ **One action I'll take**

Being crazy – the fun way!

When was the last time you surprised yourself and those around you?
In a good way, that is. Did something out of character, made fun of something you would normally take very seriously??

Well, I don't like cooking that much, but last week, as HelloFresh turned up on my doorstep, I decided to have a party that night while cooking. I closed the doors, turned up some funky music, and literally jumped and danced while preparing the meal, sniffing the herbs and ingredients like it was the first time I'd met them. Hello, Basil!! Hazardous moments? Yes. Did I end up laughing at myself for jumping and goofing around? Yes. Did the family later question whether that was me jumping before … causing the movement they felt in the floor … ?? Haha …

Surprise yourself. Surprise others. Cherish the moment. Throw a party while doing mundane daily tasks like "The Clothesline Funk" (putting a smile on the neighbours' faces too), "Cleaning the Kitchen after Dinner Dance", the "Finding a Way Through to the Floor Tidying Up Tango".

"Dance with the Kids Just Because You Can" is another great one because they may stop joining in when high school hits and only focus on what others think (well, let's tackle that one another day!).

Some of these chores we need to do no matter what. So why not make them fun? What is your crazy idea? Start at home, safely, before venturing into the "Waiting at the Copier Hip Hop". Funk on!

⭐ **Reflections?**

⭐ **One action I'll take**

Creating our ideal average day

Not the Facebook moments, the average ones

Jeg holder af hverdagen.

Hverdagen. Google translate it. The blog title is inspired by Dan Turell's *Jeg holder af hverdagen* about cherishing everyday life. It's what we've got most of.

I think of it as stacks of pictures pop up in my social media feed from holiday destinations around Europe: the family at dinner in another country, doing family activities together, relaxing by a resort pool, and so on. The emotions conveyed are happiness, contentment, love, joy. Very real, and very heartfelt.

Here's my message. How can you recreate these emotions around the Monday night dinner table? Make sure to do things together on a Wednesday? Take time out to relax on a Thursday?

Most people spend more time planning for their next holiday than creating the everyday life they want. What is your ideal average day? The day that you would want to live again and again, experiencing the emotions you want: happiness, contentment, love, joy ...

What most people are not aware of is that you CAN create your ideal average day. By making a conscious decision today (yes, today! — take 30 minutes out to write down your ideal day). Because as you decide what really would be your ideal (not your family's or your friends' — but YOUR ideal), and you write it down, you can start making little

5% adjustments in your everyday life that will allow you to have MORE of those moments and experience exactly the feelings you want.

Where would you live? What would your house look like? And be honest with yourself. You may prefer a small, cosy, easy-to-keep place – why then aim for a big place that requires hours of maintenance?? What would you have for breakfast? What's the view like? What's the conversation about? What does the mundane stuff look like (because it will always be there)? Who are your friends? You get the gist.

So, cherish the holidays and weekends away. Notice the kind of experiences that make you happy and content. And then consciously look for how you can create little moments that produce exactly THOSE feelings in your everyday life.

Enjoy *hverdagen*. It's worth it. You're worth it …

★ **Reflections?**

★ **One action I'll take**

What makes your heart sing?

A weekend of singing. With 40 awesome people. Practising for our upcoming gig. But also enjoying great conversations — getting to know the newer members we haven't had a chance to talk to yet and getting closer to those we already know. Singing, grooving, eating, laughing, dancing, playing games. While getting SO ready and pumped for the performance. Do I feel like the luckiest person ever?

What makes YOUR heart sing? What brings you joy and energy?

What can you bring into your everyday life, your work, your business? To balance out the things that may not be that easy at the moment.

Having a hobby is a great thing. Making time for it is YOUR responsibility. If this is stirring your pot, find out what it could be for you, and how to make it happen before the end of the year. Your future self will thank you for it.

★ Reflections?

★ One action I'll take

What's worse: lying to others or to yourself?

In our family, we use a quote from my father-in-law: "You can lie to others but not to yourself." (In Danish, "*man kan lyve for alle andre men ikke for sig selv.*") It made me wonder, what's worse: lying to others or to yourself? Or lying full stop?

My family upbringing was more around total honesty and not lying to anyone at all — but with life experience, I realise that we do lie. Mostly small white lies to not upset people, but there are those people who live their lives with big lies. Some are very aware of being honest and upfront with others — but lie to their true selves by not listening to their own needs or standing up for themselves and what is important to them.

I guess the meaning of his quote is that we, deep down, know what's right for us, and that we get hints when we're not living in a way that is true to our own values and purpose.

The other side of the coin of honesty versus lies is that when we are honest, we can hurt people as well, so is that actually better than lying? I have dished out more than my fair share of hurt by being honest and not being able to hide emotions. So, I've had to learn to lie — or as I prefer to put it: I tell the truth but have realised I don't need to give all the details or tell a long story. Phrase things so you are honest with both yourself and the person on the receiving end. And you don't need to speak all you think and know. Choose wisely with a filter of whether it will be helpful or not for the other person. Lots of learning for me still …

I truly believe, though, that lying or covering up doesn't serve any purpose at all. Yes, sometimes the truth is painful, both for us and for others. But sometimes being vulnerable and honest opens up a totally different level of conversation – as long as the truth is said with respect and we stick around for the conversation, not throwing it as a stink bomb and running off … Covering it up just delays the learning.

What's your view here? Honesty before everything else? Telling the truth as constructively as possible? Or lying and delaying the realisation of what's really going on?

Can I be guaranteed another 46 years minimum to practise??
That would be great, thanks.

★ **Reflections?**

★ **One action I'll take**

Time management to perfection – including time to relax!

Planning ahead can keep you out of most trouble. You knew that, didn't you? When you get super stressed and angry at everyone in traffic, it's really because you left 15 minutes later than planned, right? So count backwards, and get the things you REALLY need to get done, done in time. And then DON'T start seven other things that you just thought of and may be able to pull off. Don't be a time optimist — be a time realist. Then YOU will be happier.

And when you know that you get really grumpy if you don't get any food for hours, then make sure to always have some carrot sticks or almonds/raisins in your bag. I must look like a hamster, always bringing food — and starting the morning by laying out my small snacks at my desk. But, uh, I tell you: it's for the good of all of us!!

Don't use planning as an excuse to get even more stressed (and stress others out). There were some mornings when my husband actually asked me to get out of there — because I was planning, managing, shooting out orders … and stressing them all out.

So, how to use this skill to make time for the IMPORTANT things? So many of us manage it to perfection when it's about getting kids ready for school on time or getting that work project delivered on time. But when was the last time that you planned to perfection in order to get time to just do YOUR thing?

A colleague was offering half an hour of meditation for a group of us every fortnight. There would have been enough excuses to not be able to go, but I really wanted to try it out and make it happen. And then you realise how many of the "fixed" things you can actually make fluid. How agendas and meetings can be adjusted, made short and to the point, and how you can plan to get that half an hour fitted in.

Well, I'm not a doctor dealing with life and death situations – but, really, most of us aren't. We just think our work is life or death. Anyway, that half an hour every fortnight has been a real blessing. Learning how to relax, my way, to the most serene, inspiring visualisations – and coming back after half an hour with new energy worth HOURS.

So think of this: keep fine-tuning your planning and time management skills to make everything run more smoothly because you have thought and planned ahead. And then make sure to plan for some time for just YOU every week. Enjoy planning!

★ **Reflections?**

★ **One action I'll take**

That awesome fifth day?!

You clever ones out there working four days a week. Can you do something for the team (that's the rest of us, still working five days a week, and the poor souls working even more!!)?

Spend the fifth day intentionally on all the things that will create the future YOU. On the things you need to learn more about or practise or that will push you out of your comfort zone (no, vacuuming does not count!). So, to become the person you really want to become, you MUST spend your fifth day off preparing 100% for that, as if it's a matter of life or death!

Ready? Three rules apply:

Rule #1: You have to do the vacuuming and washing during the four days you work, as if you were full-time! When you really know what you want to change in you and in your life, how wasteful would it be after a month to have vacuumed your house four times? Versus having read, watched YouTube videos, or networked with people who already role model what you want to become – imagine the difference in you!

Rule #2: Start today and spend at least four weeks thinking differently, pushing up against your comfort zone, going to relevant networking events (and TALKING with strangers; if you go and stay in a corner, you might as well have stayed in bed!). Imagine how many new thoughts you will have had after four weeks, and how many new actions you will have taken. Refreshing!

Rule #3: Focus on your passion. NOW. No excuses. What are you passionate about? Who do you want to become? Start thinking about it, and focus on it NOW. You will find the teachers and role models you need when you look up from that washing basket (or ... insert whatever you use as an excuse to procrastinate!).

When you have become excellent at investing in YOU on your fifth day, you can mix it up again and create a win-win situation: you study stuff online from when the kids leave for school at 8 (study, I said, not check Facebook!), and when you then hang up the washing at 10, you will get SO many great ideas and the learning will settle in. Whereas if you had only done the washing, your thoughts would have been exactly the same as yesterday (and the day before, and the day before ...). It is only when you reach this level – and this is important – that you are allowed to incorporate homely chores into your fifth day.

And now the twist – of COURSE this applies to YOU as well, working full-time, busy schedule, blah-blah ... You just thought you were off the hook, right? One more rule for you.

Rule #4: Dedicate at least six hours a week just to YOU. To your passions and to opportunities to stretch beyond your busy comfort zone. Yes, I know you can — and you know it too.

Ready? Set. GO!!!!

★ **Reflections?**

★ **One action I'll take**

Just stay home one weekend — just one.

How come some people think it's OK to say yes to an invite – and then when the day comes, they drop out? I've seen this happen quite a lot here, and my Danish heart goes: *That's not ON!* When you say yes, it's a yes – no excuses. Even better: say NO. It's OK – you probably know you won't have time/energy/feel like it, so be honest up front and decline.

Do you know what's much better? PLAN for a weekend with nothing on now and then. And driving kids to this and that does count: teach them to take the bike/bus/walk or ask another parent to carpool and take turns. You don't NEED to be on the sidelines every weekend. Really. You don't.

And I'm not being mean here – I enjoy watching my kids' activities, being there to support them and see how they're doing. But don't ever use it as an excuse. It's your choice – and it's OK to plan a weekend off.

You may have guessed my kids now have two digits in their ages. But even with small kids, you would be amazed how much they would enjoy watching and joining you in something you are really passionate about one weekend, without the oozing bitterness and "all-the-things-I-have-to-do-stress", which definitely will make them fight and moan to get attention.

Back to this empty weekend idea. Don't invite people over. Don't go shopping (WHAT?? Starve the family??). Dig deeper in the cupboards/

fridge/freezer, and get creative with what you've got (omelette a la ...?!). Buy milk, a loaf of bread, and a bag of apples from the corner store. Money and time saved right there. So, do things YOU want to do, that give you energy and make you happy (what a strange concept!!).

I bet you don't dare! Because the REALLY scary thing is having time. And not knowing how to spend it when all excuses don't count. So, it may take a few "free weekends" before you can hear that inner voice and know exactly what you would actually like to do.

Hey ... *psst* ... when you get itchy feet because you have nothing on, don't start harassing the rest of the family about what they should do. Just let everyone follow their hearts, just this weekend.

★ **Reflections?**

★ **One action I'll take**

Washing clothes — is it that time of year again?

We do two to four loads of washing on the weekend. That's it. You may think we wear dirty clothes. Well, no, we just dig deeper in the drawers, and the kids wear the smaller-size uniforms they don't really like until the next sunny day. We're also smart about using layers, so you only change the small tops underneath and reuse the outer layers. And some weekends, we don't wash at all — by choice (see blog 18 on choice!).

You will also survive not having clean linen on the beds every week/month/quarter (insert your current benchmark). Believe me. And you can live a healthy life with some dirt and spots in your life. As for sports clothes: some can be worn twice (yes!). And if it's the kids' sports clothes piling up: teach them to put a load on themselves. Much better.

Four years or so back, when colleagues on a Monday were discussing their Mother's Day outings and the amazing cafes they'd been to, I (proudly!) proclaimed that I had made it the BEST Mother's Day ever — by getting the kids to do all the washing. They had tried it before, but this Sunday, I sat on my hands — or more precisely with a book — within a safe distance to the laundry and asked them to do the whole thing themselves: sorting, washing, hanging it up. They could come and ask questions, and they did a few times, but they did it all themselves!

So, do you see my point of it being the best Mother's Day gift ever? How many hours and days did that give me in all future years to do

MY passions (see blog seven and eight on finding your passion)?? Of course, we adults do the washing as well (and I now actually enjoy it instead of seeing it as a burden), but it's absolutely our responsibility to get the kids doing it as well! And on that Mother's Day, we did also go to a cafe in the afternoon when the washing was done …

Kids actually DO want to help (even if they moan at first). You know yourself how great it feels when you can deal with something and the sense of empowerment it gives you — kids are no different! But that's for another day:-)

★ **Reflections?**

★ **One action I'll take**

What I really want for Christmas ...

... is to take myself less seriously!! What a great gift! My husband has been trying to give that exact gift to me ever since we got back together as adults. But you know how it goes when you get something you don't want. Imagine the face, the polite, stiff smile ... but everyone can see that this gift is NOT what you had in mind.

I grew up in a family where we actually got things from our wish list. Why ask for a list if you are going to buy other stuff YOU think they want? Then don't ask for a wish list. Well, as a consequence, in my family, we wrote lovely long wish lists for birthdays and Christmas – and indeed got something from our list every time. How is that for teaching your kids to wish for what they really want?

Anyway, I have gotten side-tracked here. Back to the decades of receiving a gift I had NOT wished for: humour. Even worse: being nudged to laugh at myself!! So I politely returned it. Didn't even unwrap it.

And now, suddenly, mid-life, what do I find myself wanting? To laugh more, especially at myself. To ask fewer questions and not add comments that come from the head when the rest of the family is having a great laugh.

Laughing a lot more. About silly things. Including myself – especially myself, actually. It is SO entertaining. And what makes me really happy? Listening to the rest of the family laughing, with belly laughs, just

BEING, joining in. Not commenting, analysing, seeing the other side. How appropriate that we just watched Mrs Doubtfire!!

Oh dear. This year, I may just get what I REALLY want. Ho-ho-ho … a hilarious year ahead. I'm going in!!

★ **Reflections?**

★ **One action I'll take**

Shifting our language and mindset

Put into words what you want to make happen

21

All emotions welcome ... oh, noooooo!!

We grow up learning not to cry, not to be angry, to be a good boy/girl. And guess what? We teach our own kids the same thing. Because it's so much easier (read: I've got things under control) when people around us behave calmly, politely, and mostly happily.

The thing is: we HAVE all kinds of emotions. All the time. And it's OK to have them. So, start welcoming them. In yourself. In others. "Wow, you're angry – that's really important to you, isn't it?" (Just try to say it to yourself/others without sounding condescending. It's meant well, try coming from your heart when you say it.)

So, when things fall apart. When you are sad, angry, alone, have had enough. Accept it. It's OK. Own your emotions. They are exactly that: YOUR emotions. No one else's. Accept them, however ugly and unattractive they may seem in the moment.

They are your emotions. Signals to you that something has to change. In you. In the standards you set for others or yourself. In what you say yes to (or should have said no to?). Go explore. All of your emotions. They pop up for a reason. So, explore with curiosity and wonder.

There is no "think happy thoughts" platitude that solves it all. Listen and act on what needs to be acted on. That will make you feel better. But forcing yourself to feel good without changing the root cause is just delaying trouble. Off you go exploring … ooooh, a tiny bit scary and exciting at the same time, isn't it? Happy Sunday.

★ **Reflections?**

★ **One action I'll take**

22

"Don't think of a pink elephant." I said, "DON'T think of a pink elephant."

Did you know ... our brains don't pick up NOTs and DON'Ts? So when you say (out loud or just to yourself inside your head) "I don't want to be tired", the only thing registered is "I want to be tired". Pick a few typical examples from your arsenal of self-talk – come on, I know you have a few standard ones!

Let's try an experiment. Don't think of a pink elephant. Don't think of a pink elephant.

Which image immediately flicked through your head? Your brain needs to create the image of the pink elephant before it can add the "don't". Do you see the trouble that's creating?

You may have heard that what you focus on is what you get. It's the law of attraction. The more you think and talk about something, the more it comes to mind. The more attention you give it, the more of it you get.

So the more you talk and think about how tired you are ... Guess what? You feel even more tired! So while exactly that will be mentioned a lot in a mothers' group, and when one says it, the others need to trump it with stories of how they are even MORE tired ... it may support the feeling of belonging, but it definitely doesn't make anyone feel more energised!

The sum of all the "I'm so tired" and "I don't want to feel so tired" moments add up to a lot. So use your language wisely: to create what you want, what you want more of — what you want to attract. Sounds simple, right?

Here's a funny exercise for you until next time: start listening for all the times you say or think what you DON'T want or what you are NOT. Then immediately change it into what you WANT or ARE. How cool is that? I tell you, it will change what you focus on — and what you get.

Why just take my word for it? Test it out. Have some FUN chasing the negatively loaded words in your OWN language and swap them for positive ones (haha … you were just ready for a verbal attack on friends and family — what about leading by example instead?). Or you may have to swap positive ones if they are hiding the emotion you really need to face (I'm not happy. What are you then? Why and what to do about it? Learn more about owning your emotions in blog 24). The brain doesn't pick up negations.

Watch your thoughts; they become your language. Watch your language; it becomes your actions. Watch your actions; they become your habits. (And remember to have fun!)

★ **Reflections?**

★ **One action I'll take**

The little BUT ...

I read an article the other day that reminded me of the word BUT. It's one of the first changes you make when you start becoming aware of language — whether as a coach, a parent, or a leader. To replace BUT in all your sentences with AND.

It seems like a tiny thing, and yet, it has a profound effect. Try it. A compliment, a positive comment about the party you were at or the person you were talking with — and then you add another sentence and link them with BUT. "She is really nice, but she talks a lot."

Immediately, you have diminished, deleted, negated anything positive you have just said — the person on the receiving end concludes that it was just nice wrapping; now comes the real message.

With a but, it is implied that talking a lot is not a good thing. You pick up that she's viewed in a negative light because of it. Now, see how a tiny change can have a positive effect: "She is really nice, and she talks a lot." Do you see how the judgment has diminished? It can be positive, or no matter how we perceive it, it's accepted as who she is. It could mean that she's good at connecting with others — and even if it's not your thing, you don't fault or judge her for it.

If we go deeper, it's about judgment. Even if not intended that way, we judge the situation and the other person — and make them just that bit smaller, less accepted, less lovable.

So, start removing it from your language. Become aware of how often you belittle or judge. And instead of diminishing with BUT, practise expanding with AND.

Enjoy the next blog, and enjoy expanding others.

⭐ **Reflections?**

⭐ **One action I'll take**

Me ... butthurt?! The four steps to owning your own stuff.

What's the worst version of yourself? In the moments you're not proud of, the ones not shared on social media. Is it when you're bitter, angry, sad, lonely, or maybe, like me, butthurt? That last one, butthurt, was my family describing me. *Ouch …*

We tend to have a version of ourselves that we present to others. And then we have the other side. The parts of ourselves that we have shame or embarrassment around because they are not as attractive to others, based on our conclusions from life so far.

The trick to emotional intimacy is, as for all other things, practice.

Why would we want to practise it? To accept that all emotions are good signals for us — they don't need to be sorted into a list of good and bad emotions. And they don't need to be shared with others as we practise. When learning the piano, we have a go ourselves before we take it to the concert hall, right?

As we get more aware of all our emotions and allow them to show, they don't scare us anymore — whether they are coming from ourselves or others.

Let's get clear on this: becoming intimate with our emotions is not about wallowing in them, creating dramas around them, or suddenly bucketing them over others. It's about putting on our explorer's hat and, with deep, innate curiosity, having a look at them, feeling them, getting to know them. As if you were practising scales on the piano.

That's the way forward. Instead of our usual way (for all of us!) of hiding the emotions, pushing them away, pretending they're not there, or being so afraid of them that we have stopped having them all together. Imagine learning to play the piano, but only allowing yourself to use three of the white keys. We would miss out on a lot.

Back to me. So, I noticed how the family mentioned me getting butthurt. The definition of butthurt is "overly or unjustifiably offended or resentful". But more than expanding our emotional vocabulary by looking it up, it's about exploring inwards with curiosity.

This is the exercise for you to do – with your "go-to reactions" that are not serving you. I've done it. Many times. And it works.

The four steps are:

- ★ **Name it** (In this case: I feel butthurt!)
- ★ **Own it** (Ooops ... It's not what they said or did. It's MY feeling, my stuff coming up)
- ★ **FEEL it** (Give it some curious explorer's hat time. What's that really about, when I'm butthurt? How is my inner critic adding to the pity

party? What is it I didn't get in that moment that I would have liked to get? Where in the body can I feel it – how does it feel?)

★ **Let it be** (DON'T hide it or push it away – accept it)

This can be a one-minute exploration in your mind. Or a twenty-minute journey of discovery. The key is that YOU decide when and where to explore it – and you decide when to pause the exploration.

If you're blank on which emotion to start looking for first, over the next week, be aware of when you defend yourself. Or times when you apply an advanced counter-attack tactic. What was the emotion you felt there, right before lashing out (or pulling away)? That's the one to explore.

My keys on the piano are expanding. With my explorer's hat on, I've now become familiar with butthurt (oh, hello … is it you again? Welcome!). Sadness has been allowed in too. And the emotion I have most avoided – anger – has been real fun to practise with myself. For real.

And this is, of course, the key: whatever emotions we don't like or accept in others are the emotions we don't like or accept in ourselves. Own it.

This led me to profoundly apologise to my husband for trying to stop and block his healthy versions of anger, which I've resented for the last twenty years. I now know when the time is right for feeling angry about something — and no one else may ever know, because it's not about that outward reaction, it's about owning it and listening to the signal it's sending. Allowing ourselves to have a go at using all the keys of the piano.

In the right setting, all emotions are OK. They make our lives richer, deeper, more fully expressed. Truer. Ours.

So, what is the first emotion that you will befriend? Name it, and start the exploration. Enjoy!!

★ **Reflections?**

★ **One action I'll take**

Fear and risky vs safe problems

Keeping ourselves busy with safe problems

Honey, the kids have shrunk!

Honey, the climbing castle has shrunk! Well, as I passed my old pre-school, years later, I was shocked to see the old climbing castle had shrunk. What in my memory was a tall, towering construction with a suspension bridge hanging far above the ground was now a mere man-sized castle with a simple link from tower to tower.

As you already know, it hadn't shrunk — my perspective had changed. Have you had similar experiences?

Some things we recall, but our recollection is only a version of the actual event, with deletions, distractions, and filters based on who we were back then, and what we chose to focus on and remember.

How many things in your life are you clinging onto with an old perception, a memory, a recalled situation, that is not serving you anymore? It may be about time to take a new look at it. Get your perspective updated. You never know, it may have shrunk. Happy updating.

★ **Reflections?**

★ **One action I'll take**

'Cuse me – is that lipstick on your teeth??!

Is it just me seeing the bit of food on your nose or the lipstick on your front tooth? I know I'm definitely one of the few who will point it out!

Why don't people say it? Yes, it's a bit awkward. Having to pause the conversation. Looking at the other person until they are sure it's gone. Is it because you fear the ultimate embarrassment – that it was NOT food but a permanent skin problem?? Or that the lipstick is one of those permanent ones, so that it becomes a ten-minute struggle to get it off?

Whatever the reason is, get over yourself! If YOU think it is embarrassing pointing it out, then think of THEM two hours later, looking at themselves in the mirror and realising they have spoken to dozens of people over the last hours with whipped CREAM on their nose!! THAT is embarrassing!

Be the trusted one. Dare to help others, even – or especially – when risking making a fool of yourself.

The struggle of eating finger food gracefully in public while making conversation and holding a glass. That's something we can all relate to. That's what you can have a laugh about together – the dropped meatball is what you will remember (especially if you pick it up from the floor and eat it while saying, "Two-minute rule"!). Those who run away won't stick around anyway. And those who laugh with you could end up becoming interesting companions.

So, join me. What will YOU be spotting next time? And promise you will speak up?? Happy networking.

★ **Reflections?**

★ **One action I'll take**

Can this be returned? Please.

After people spend a manic December buying all sorts of stuff for each other, come 27 December, and it's like an old-fashioned tape recorder rewinding — or a movie in reverse. People driving, walking, BACK to the same shops, returning, swapping ...

Has anyone calculated how much time we would save as a nation if we made a law that we could only give experiences as gifts next Christmas? Just like in Denmark when they had "car-free Sundays" to make people change their behaviour (during the oil crisis in the 70s), moving towards something more sustainable — in every meaning of the word. And today (for many reasons), half of Copenhagen's population ride a bicycle to work/uni.

Back to Christmas. A Christmas free of physical presents. How much stress would we avoid? How much wrapping paper? How many litres of petrol? How many family arguments? And now add the hassle of returning, swapping, keeping-it-but-not-using-it-and-having-to-pretend-you-use-it-everytime-she-visits? How much emotional pressure would we release?

So next Christmas ... Give picnics. Give laughter. Give bike rides. Give kisses. Give joy. Give bush walks. Give hugs. And the stuff that you REALLY want and need ...

My husband answered "Peace on Earth" every time the girls asked what he wanted for Christmas. And then Secret Santa actually made it happen! This Santa, with great attention to detail, hand-painted a little ball and reproduced the Earth in green and blue – with a peace sign glued on. Plan B was creating a shoebox with green peas nicely decorating some soil. Anyway – be creative. Give what's most important to you and especially to those who receive it.

 AUTHOR'S NOTE: This continued for years after this blog was written, and the girls got more and more creative in expressing "Peace on Earth". Brilliant!

You know the saying "Treat others as you would like to be treated"? Do you know what's even better? Treat others the way THEY want to be treated. And for Christmas, give them what they really want. Mix experiences up with books, runners, undies, whatever is on their list – but check the size, and make sure it CAN be returned if it doesn't float their boat.

Let's aim at no returns.

★ **Reflections?**

★ **One action I'll take**

One foot on the brake.

Do you have one foot on the accelerator and one on the brake?

We have this Gran Turismo game that was great entertainment for our visitors and ourselves over the holidays. The thing is, you can easily have one foot on the accelerator and at the same time be braking with the other.

It reminded me of how a lot of us live our lives. Moving forward, going for it, BUT at the same time, we have the other foot on the brake. What if ... I can't ... All the fears going at the same time as we're trying to let ourselves progress.

There is a brilliant quote about success being our goals minus our fears, and that's exactly it: with a foot on the brake at the same time as the other one is trying to get us to accelerate, we won't get very far.

So, have a go at living your life NOT as if it's a game with a Gran Turismo pedal, but as if it's a manual car, where you put your foot on the accelerator and ENJOY the ride. And then, now and then, move your foot to the brake. Stop for a bit, take account of the direction, check in on your capabilities. Then move the foot back to the accelerator.

Go, girl, go.

⭐ **Reflections?**

⭐ **One action I'll take**

Generosity and empowerment

Are you a giver or a getter??

All people pleasers will feel really good and think they are a GIVER. Maybe stop reading now or brace yourself for what's coming!!

Giving is a beautiful thing, but the key is the WAY we give. Is it with slight bitterness, martyrdom, or defeat (no one else is gonna do it ...)? What if it wasn't about giving things or "services" (doing all the mundane stuff for others)? What if the best thing we could give was significance?

And here comes the crucial question: are you a giver or a getter of significance??

Significance as in making us feel seen, that we matter, that it makes a difference we're here.

So, do you GIVE others significance: being fully present in that moment, showing true interest in what others are saying, listening without prejudice or your map of right and wrong superimposed on top, asking questions to understand more?

Or are you more about GETTING significance? "See how nothing would get done here without me," topping others' stories with one you have that's even worse/bigger/better ... The full-blown significance-getters are the drama kings and queens of this world — but most of us do it way more discretely in many situations, without even being aware of it.

Start your radar scanning your own ratio of getting and giving significance this coming week. And notice how great it feels when you're really into someone else and what they're saying, doing, or even better, BEING. The silent acceptance of who we're being can be one of the strongest. That's why pottering about in the garden with a grandparent can be so lovely — no questions, just being. It can be as simple as a smile to someone you're passing — acknowledging their presence.

My parents are absolutely amazing. I've often said to my teams that everyone should spend a week with my parents. With the words I know today, I can say that they are true givers of significance. When you are with them, they are truly interested in you, they listen with open minds (most of the time, apart from when you say you're moving to the other side of the world, virtually kidnapping the grandkids … Well, we're all human!). They ask questions to understand where you're coming from or why it's important to you, and you sense their good wishes for everyone, no matter the normal external gauges of status or social acceptance. They feel good in their own skins — and therefore have the space for others.

With three cheers to my parents, let's all do our best this week to explore GIVING significance.

★ **Reflections?**

★ **One action I'll take**

OMG – am I an introvert??

Most of you, who have met me, would say no. I like being around people, like talking, and do occasionally end up being the centre of attention with a good story ... Well, well, what if it wasn't as black and white as that?

Who here treasures time on their own? Thought so. And who here needs downtime after lots of socialising? Thought so again.

We are not one or the other. And there IS no right or wrong — even if society, the schooling system, workplaces with open offices, and many other things make us believe being extroverted is the only thing that counts. It's not as simple as "Do you prefer partying or staying home alone?" How social we are may give a hint, but our preference is as much about how we motivate ourselves — do we get energy from others, from outside, or do we get our energy from within?

As always, there is value in diversity. Have you noticed how the best conversation partners are often more introverted? They actually LISTEN to what you say, as they aren't too busy talking about themselves. Often they have a deep knowledge and understanding of lots of fascinating subjects.

I'm very fortunate to be surrounded by a lovely mix of people who span the scale of extroversion and introversion. I've learnt to make things less about me (WHAT?? Yep ...!!), and truly treasure connecting deeply with one or two people through a great conversation, compared to having a quick chat with everyone present. Through this shift, my world has been constantly expanding. It's a relief to not always have to add a comment, a suggestion, or a story to top it — and to simply listen. It's great — have a go!

There is some great literature around this. One book to check out is Susan Cain's *The Power of Introverts in a World That Can't Stop Talking*. Not a walk in the park, but great for those of you really interested in the subject. An easier way to learn is to explore and observe those around you, getting curious when inspiration comes your way through a new perspective. My world expanded a few degrees by seeing this quote on a PJ top: "My favourite party trick is not going."

With humour, that quote says what it's all about: knowing what you prefer spending your time doing, and what you don't. We serve ourselves and those around us best by getting the balance right — time on our own, and time with others — and in a way that suits us.

If you're strongly extroverted, have a go at exploring your inner introvert this week. Enjoy being thoughtful, observant, and aware. And who knows? The world may start listening.

★ **Reflections?**

★ **One action I'll take**

Living selfishly (yes, that's OK!).

Hmm ... this may not be a perfect fit for a Valentine's Day post — or maybe it is exactly that!! Because to create a great life for yourself and those around you, you need to learn to live selfishly.

My mum lives to serve others. I admire that. But it works best when you back yourself at the same time. My mum does — not a lot of women do. They give and give ... but you sense that it's because they do NOT know how to put themselves first.

Here's a cliché (but clichés are around because they hold a truth and therefore have been told many times!). When flying, remember how the crew tell you to put on your OWN oxygen mask before helping children or others around you. Yep. That's exactly it. You can help others on a whole different level when you make sure your needs are met first — then it flows, overflows, and with happiness and contentment as wrapping instead of bitterness, apologies, or defeat.

Put yourself first. Just once a week. There are so many ways of doing it (with no animals or humans being harmed ...).

★ **AUTHOR'S NOTE:** re-read blogs 1, 7–11, 13, 14, 16–19. Okay, just re-read the whole start of the book, new ideas always pop up when we hear, read or think about things a second time.

"I'm not wired that way." "I don't back myself." Good news: you can learn this stuff. And it's not hard. It just takes practice. And a decision to let go of pleasing everyone. Good news: that's easy to let go of as well. A good coach can help you.

Selfishness is not always well-received. Well, honestly, it never is. You have to stand your ground and have a purpose that is important enough to fight for. I'm envisaging Colonel Hathi from Disney's *The Jungle Book*. Hup, 2, 3, 4 … Keep it up, 2, 3, 4. Thick-skinned and with a purpose. I have something important to do. Hup, 2, 3, 4 … Keep it up, 2, 3, 4. I will find a way of getting the results, no matter what comes tumbling down. Hup, 2, 3, 4 … Keep it up, 2, 3, 4. For my own fun, I've dressed up the marching patrol in my mind with happy colours and a few dance steps mixed in.

So here is my Valentine's wish for you: write a love letter to yourself this year. Ask yourself to start living selfishly – for your own good, the good of others, and the greater good.

Hup, 2, 3, 4 … Keep it up, 2, 3, 4!

★ **Reflections?**

★ **One action I'll take**

It's all a strategy

Let's get down to business

How do you brush your teeth?

Everything we do is done with a strategy. A simple example: we have a strategy for brushing our teeth. We follow some steps, and they lead to an outcome. If we want a different result from our teeth brushing, we need to change a step – and possibly get inspiration from someone getting the results we want. So, how do you brush your teeth? All we do is done with a strategy.

Brushing your teeth differently may be setting the bar a bit low. So, let's look for something meatier that you would like to do better this year. What is your strategy for that right now?

Let's say it's your relationship with those close to you (excellent choice as we all have at least one complex relationship, right??). What's your strategy for relationships? How do you "do" relationships?

Are you getting the results you want in your relationships? It's such an easy one to spot – because if we feel close and respected, if we allow each other to be who we are and give each other space and support, the relationship blossoms. We know when they are not working. And it's not your fault, or someone else's fault. It's just feedback that you're not yet allowing each other to be yourselves – feeling enough, feeling loved, feeling we matter – in the way that each one of you want to be seen.

Wow, we got deep quickly, didn't we? We talked about this one in blog 27: "Treat others as you would like to be treated." It's NOT true.

The ultimate truth is we should treat others as THEY would like to be treated. And because we're all different, it takes a lot of listening and curiosity to start understanding how to really make each other light up.

So, how are you doing relationships? Being aware that it's not something happening TO us, but that we have a choice in how we do it, is so powerful. We could stop right here. Place that thought in the front of your mind and heart over the coming weeks and months and things will start changing for you in surprising and wonderful ways.

If you need to change something about your strategy, look for role models who are already getting the results you want. Try out some of their steps. Because as soon as you change ONE little step in your current strategy, things cannot end up as they normally do – something will change. If it's not enough or things are not moving in the right direction, make another little change and keep it going for a while.

Some of you may feel cheated that you can't blame it on others. It may be a struggle to accept, but when you give in to the belief that it is a choice, it is AWESOME, because when all we do is done with a strategy, we have the CHOICE to look for different results by doing things differently.

Personally, I've done a lot of work this year on "how I do playful" – and I'm getting to a pretty good strategy that works for me. Related to playful, I want to shout a heartfelt thank you for reading, applying, and enjoying my posts and short stories. I truly appreciate the feedback I'm getting from so many of you: it's such a joy to inspire your journeys, in whatever way we connect and grow together. This truly makes me want to continue writing and sharing, which is one of the ways I "do playful". Thank you.

So, what's your thing to work on for YOU the coming twelve months? And if nothing pops up, just enjoy brushing your teeth this coming week … and months … It's all a strategy.

★ Reflections?

★ One action I'll take

Sushi train
of thoughts.

We all have around 70,000 thoughts a day. No wonder it can get a bit overwhelming! The beauty is, though, that it doesn't matter how many thoughts we have flying past — what matters is which ones we grab and hang onto, take for a spin, ponder, and let linger. They are the ones that risk dragging us down or help to bring us up.

Recently, a really refreshing tactic came from a Danish team successfully working to help people with depression, and it is a tactic we can all learn from: limit the amount of time a day that you dive into and ruminate on worrying thoughts.

Aha! It's NOT changing negative thoughts into positive ones. It's NOT trying to empty your mind and not think at all (how can we possibly, with 70,000 thoughts a day?). It's limiting the amount of time we allow ourselves to give the worrying thoughts attention.

Specifically, set a time that becomes your routine "worrywart time". Let's say 8–9pm every day. Whenever you catch yourself jumping onto the worry train, jump off — you will worry about it at 8pm (and, no, you do not need to write a note about it).

Simplified, it's observing your thoughts like a sushi train. Noticing the plates of salmon sashimi, tempura, and tiger rolls pass by. And realising you don't HAVE to grab them. Let them stay on the train. They may even come back a second time; you still don't have to grab them.

In this case, with your new 8–9pm worrywart slot, you can wait until then, and see if any of them pop up and still have your interest by then.

This goes for your own mind as well as the collective mind in your teams and your business. We have a choice – about which thoughts and discussions we pick up, and which ones we park for later. How liberating to let the worrying wait. "You're not controlling me. I'm in charge, and I decide when and for how long I jump on your train."

Enjoy practising jumping off the worry train this coming week.

★ **Reflections?**

★ **One action I'll take**

Asking myself what??

The quality of our lives is determined by the quality of the questions we ask ourselves. Unfortunately, most of us ask ourselves really rubbish questions.

You know how great leaders ask great questions – instead of just telling people what to do, which is a common but low standard of leadership?

Well, for all of us, leaders of businesses, teams – and leaders of life – most of the questions we ask never pass our lips. They are part of the constant self-talk in our heads, the looping noise.

Starting the day with (self-talk) questions like "How am I going to manage all this?" or "Why me?" or "How am I going to get through this day?" is pretty common, even for the best of us. But we give our brains very little chance of high-quality answers with such a low starting point. Our brain's best options would be answering "You're not," "Because that's what always happens," and "Barely breathing."

So, what about setting the bar a little higher? A good place to start is with these seven quality questions that give your brain an opportunity to actually look for a quality answer (they are *The Morning Power Questions* from Tony Robbins' *Awaken the Giant Within*). You must do them fast, no pondering, so it really just takes a few minutes – with an OK side effect of starting the day by creating new neural pathways.

Here we go:

1. What am I happy about [in my life right now]?
    a. What about it makes me happy?
    b. How does that make me feel?
2. What am I excited about [...]?
    a. What about it excites me?
    b. How does that make me feel?
3. What am I proud about [...]?
    a. ...
    b. ...
4. What am I grateful about [...]?
5. What am I enjoying most [...]?
6. What am I committed to [...]?
7. Who do I love, and who loves me [...]?

Note the questions on your phone, learn them by heart, however you learn best – just do it. You will be surprised by the quality answers popping up in your brain.

Here's to a high-quality week!

★ **Reflections?**

★ **One action I'll take**

Bringing structure to our life

Not more to-do lists!

I love my morning jog. You what??

Yep, getting up half an hour earlier than needed. Getting into the slightly smelly gear from yesterday morning (remember blog 19 about washing?). Jogging through the surrounding streets and then doing 10 minutes of stretching in the street when I get back. Highly recommended!!

Do you need me to start listing the advantages? Having half an hour to yourself at the beginning of the day, no one asking you questions. Aaaaaah. Then there's the fact it's actually healthy, and you get your body to wake up – it could even just be a five-minute walk up and down the street. Some of your greatest thoughts and solutions to stuff will appear out of the blue – literally. And then you get to know all your neighbours as a bonus – the wave, the hello, while you stretch that leg on a street pole more or less gracefully. Hahaaaa … at least you give them a smile and something to laugh at to start their day!

On weekends, I jog into the bush. No phone. Just my space. So peaceful and good for the soul. I've even come to learn about a few native plants and animals as a freebie. I've also started talking to the wallabies (small kangaroos) now and then. Sorry, kids. Harming your social standing with my too-honest shares. Speaking to animals and trees doesn't give street cred.

Anyway, when I say jog, I mean jog. A really slow jog. And sometimes, I don't feel like going more than half a kilometre before I turn around. If anyone was watching, they would think I had forgotten my key, returning two minutes after I left ... haha ... But I do it for ME, so no big deal. And I never skip the stretching – that's my layman's version of meditation made simple.

Did I always feel like it? NO! But I just kept doing it, and now my body and brain don't fight it anymore. I just get on with it. And those days when I skip it for whatever reason, the proof comes later that day ... being more grumpy and tired, starting to annoy the family with things they should do. So ... whenever I start stressing and bossing others around, I know it's time to go out for a jog and let them get on with their lives uninterrupted. Win-win-win!

★ **Reflections?**

★ **One action I'll take**

Who says carrots are not a meal??

One of our daughters is at a Steiner school with lovely kids, teachers, and parents, and as we were helping out with props and sewing today for the upcoming musical, I found myself out of my league during the lunch break.

Homemade lentil soups, salads, and … talk about foods I don't even know the existence of! And there I was with my (aluminium-foil-wrapped — oh noooooo) sandwich with cheese and vacuum-packed ham, drinking water out of a reused PET bottle. Hahaaaaaa — they may not even have noticed, but I suddenly got another benchmark for living a life with healthy food and a smaller environmental footprint.

A year ago, I would have been even further out of my league, but luckily, I have discovered "HelloFresh", and our (eating) lives have never been the same since. Beautiful fresh ingredients in exact amounts, recipe steps to follow, and therefore a fully risk-free dive into cooking healthy, awesome-looking, culturally diverse dinners with the family. The kids take turns on the cooking team, chopping away at all the exotic vegetables we wouldn't be able to name if it weren't for the pictures on the recipes. And those of us not on the cooking roster automatically clean up the whole thing afterwards. A beautiful system!

For nearly twenty years, I have been very honest about cooking not being one of my fortes (alongside cleaning) and have scraped by in the dinner department with "chicken with rice and carrots" alternated with "beef with pasta and carrots" with the odd day of "stir-fry" (= emptying the fridge. Our daughters still claim some PTSD about stir-fries). I was absolutely happy with the status quo, accepting the lay of the land.

Then I met HelloFresh. And one evening shortly after, as we sat down at the dinner table, my husband took the first bite and pronounced an earnest acknowledgement of how great it tasted. Much to my surprise, big tears started running down my cheeks!! We all burst out laughing – but in that moment, my old belief of "it's good enough as it is" was blown out of the water. Tears were flowing, so it obviously HAD been much more important to me than I had admitted to myself. Being able (or not!) to cook a nice-tasting meal for the family.

So, one step at a time, I'm getting closer to appreciating the nutrition and benefits of well-cooked, varied meals. My family knows how dearly I hold the weekly box – it is three guaranteed successful meals, and then the other four nights, we are absolutely fine with toasties, omelette, pizza, yoghurt, or whatever else we can rustle up. We now have a system that's working!

Today at the Steiner school lunch, I learned what my next benchmark is: creating healthy food for me and my family for the other meals of the day too. Warning, warning: aluminium-foil-packed-ham-and-cheese sandwiches, your time is short-lived. Thank you for the simplicity and daily joy so far, but I'm going for the next level.

★ **Reflections?**

★ **One action I'll take**

Letting go – or go away for a week or two.

Little did I know that all my (well-intended) efforts to get the family to eat healthy and exercise more were in vain. I pushed and pleaded. I was the example. I poked and annoyed them all. And then went away for two weeks for work.

Leading up to my departure, the rest of the family were having visions about a dinner plan alternating between McD, Subway, and pizza, with NO carrots in sight (read my previous blog and you will know why), eating in front of the TV every night, and that's what they went with.

Returning — with a slight fear of seeing a family with their teeth falling out and pimples all over their pale faces — I was amazed to be welcomed by the happiest bunch ever! They'd had no one harassing them, and everything had flowed smoothly.

I realised that you can only set goals for yourself and lead with your example. But you can't force the horse to drink. You can help them put words to what healthy means for them — and what they could fancy doing that might be fun. But don't think YOUR ideas and ways are right for everyone else. It's not all about your checklist. Point taken.

The happy ending is that over the following months, they actually started their own ways of healthier living — so maybe TV dinners and two weeks of fast food (OK, one cooked meal, I think) weren't that inspiring either.

★ Reflections?

★ One action I'll take

Wealth buckets and I-am-ness

My self-worth is my net-worth

A trusting matter?

Big words: vulnerability, compassion, and trust. But as you know, how we do the small things is how we do everything. So, let's bring the big words into the small things in everyday life and leadership.

It's worth doing a self-study of how much you trust others – which means, how much you trust yourself.

The Scandinavian countries are at the top of the list with 68% of the population trusting others – with most other countries scoring in the 30s or even lower (from Stephen Covey's *The Speed of Trust*). This high level of trust impacts the quality of relationships and, to many people's surprise, also the tangible results of speed and cost: the more trust there is present in a relationship, a team, an organisation, or a country, the faster we are able to get things done – with the least trouble and costs, financially, and emotionally.

So, where are you on the scale of trusting others (which comes back to trusting yourself)? Do you trust yourself enough to share with vulnerability and compassion – and trust others to receive in the same way? Do you trust yourself and others enough to delegate and follow up with clear expectations? And in both instances, do you trust yourself enough to continue doing so even when the reaction is not as expected from the start?

Most people are expecting you to do to them what has already been done, which is often not a pretty picture. We're all wounded or hurt in some way — which is reflected in the low trust results for most countries.

Start surprising your team or someone you care about this coming week. Show them trust. And then continue doing it. That's you being vulnerable — and bringing a bit more compassion to your life and leadership. A trusting matter, indeed.

★ **Reflections?**

★ **One action I'll take**

39

You can't afford it? Well, well ... how much STUFF do you buy??

Let's talk about the endless stuff you spend money on today that you could stop buying. Not only would you save money – I bet you would also save time. How good is that for a win-win?

How much did you spend on takeaway because none of you thought about dinner until it was too late? On work lunches you wandered off to buy (amazing how needing lunch can surprise us every day!). On impulse-bought clothes/bags/shoes that you don't REALLY need? How much time did you spend shopping? Only great if you love Westfield or online shopping more than you love your passion. Yes, that's me checking in on whether you took action after blogs 7 and 8 and have got going with a hobby!

How easy is it for money to just evaporate? Get a financial advisor – we did! How boring and grown up does that sound?? Well, I know ours has saved us not only money but arguments and sleepless nights.

We had created quite an economic mess by moving to the other side of the world. Then this guy asked some key questions on goals and our mindsets around money. Hey, he even made me cry when asking whether we wanted to retire in Forster. (No offence, Forster. Back then, that was just the saddest thing I could imagine – and there were a few other uncovered reasons behind the tears, I realised.)

It's quite simple. You need to spend less than you earn every month. And start saving up for those big things, every month. And most of what you call FIXED costs are not at all – it's just your mindset that's fixed. About all the things you and the family NEED and the brands you HAVE to have because of your job/friends/you-name-it. So, you can afford what's important to you. Just become aware – and make some choices.

Imagine all the weekends with time for your PASSIONS (which are most likely free – or which you'll now be able to pay for!). Beautiful – how can you afford NOT to?

★ **Reflections?**

★ **One action I'll take**

You are so beautiful ... Who me??!

We all look different. Isn't that fascinating? Think of all the people you know and have ever met. That's actually a lot when you think of it! It would be hundreds, if not thousands when you add up those at school, activities you've done, concerts you've been to, and the number of people we see as we walk through the shopping centre …

As you're now mentally scanning all of those faces and bodies, do you notice how we all look different? Each one of us is our own version indeed!

So how come we have a singular, narrow idea of what beautiful is?? How come most of us aren't happy with how we look? We can start blaming the media, but what if that's really just an excuse we use to move attention away from ourselves??

Instead of accepting and trying to be happy with our bodies and looks, we create some impossible standard to measure ourselves against. That none of us will ever meet. Because every single one of us looks different. And beauty, therefore, cannot be nailed to one thing. Wow …

So let's start singing Joe Cocker's song to ourselves: "You are so beautiful … to me"! And let ourselves feel what it's like when we tell ourselves that we're beautiful. And as we all look different, let's spare ourselves the hardship of trying to look like everyone else.

So this month: every day, look yourself in the mirror (the visor mirror in the car counts as well!) and say it out loud. And when your brain goes all sarcastic on you, say it again with kindness and notice how it feels.

It probably will push some buttons. Call in a coach if you need a helping hand, and enjoy exploring what your days could be like when you accept you are what you are!!

"To be beautiful means to be yourself. You don't need to be accepted by others. You need to accept yourself." Thich Nhat Hanh.

★ **Reflections?**

★ **One action I'll take**

Saying NO.
Plainly NO.

It's Christmas soon.

 AUTHOR'S NOTE: wow, a lot of Christmas themed blogs did make the cut, didn't they? Haha … I must have been truly inspired and written good stuff around that time each year. Back to the point, and if you're reading this in February, stay with me metaphorically: It's Christmas soon.

And we say yes to everything and forget to enjoy the magic moments leading up to this lovely season. The time is right for a lesson in saying NO.

A colleague years ago told me how schools in the Netherlands had started teaching girls in year 3 to say NO. With amazing effects on the number of teenage pregnancies and rape – because the girls know how to say no, and the boys know that no means no.

So I'm going to teach you. Choose a person you trust to practise this with. Look them straight in the eyes and say NO! If you look away, smile, add a giggle or any other distraction, it doesn't count – you've just negated the whole thing. Go again.

NO! Keep practising. Say it louder and with even more conviction: *NO!!!* If you need help, add a stomp of your foot while you shout NO!

This is surprisingly difficult for many of us. Keep going. We did it with our youngest at some point, and she responded that they were not allowed to say no or talk back at an adult. That really scared me. If that is what Authority Australia teaches our kids at school, we need to get some Scandinavian values included: that your opinion matters, and that you can always speak up, no matter how many seniors are around.

So, we practised, and she got it after a while. Do it now. You can do it in an empty room, but I tell you, you need a real person in front of you, eye to eye, to test that you can do it.

When you've practised shouting it loudly, stomping and all, it becomes easier to say the little no's as well. Politely, respectfully, calmly, while keeping eye contact and standing your ground. And guess what you're teaching others by doing that? That it's OK for them to say no too.

Merry Christmas! Follow your heart and say no to those things that are not right. To those things that do not need to get done. Or do not need to get done by you. To those traditions or expectations not serving you anymore. Invite others to do the same. Accept no. And a no from others doesn't mean you need to do it instead – you can say no too.

Stop. Breathe. Bare feet on the grass.

AUTHOR'S NOTE: Me again. This applies to Australian Christmas. For the northern hemisphere, you may want to wear boots?!!

Sit with a cup of tea for five minutes.

Happy holidays.

★ **Reflections?**

★ **One action I'll take**

From ambition-driven to meaning-driven

Letting go of all the external benchmarks

I want it NOW!

Whether it's well-behaved children, a promotion, a new car, a partner we love, or our dream house – we want it NOW!

What if all those external things (including what other people do and how that make us feel) are not what it's really about? That it was never about that?!

It was never about the promotion. It was always about how you imagined you would feel when you HAD the promotion. And guess what? There is a MUCH easier way; you can choose to feel exactly that way now. Right now. Over something you already have present in your life, big or small. Go figure!

How many hours and sleepless nights have you saved right there? How much worry and guilt?

Get your gratitude journal going. In your mind, or even better, in writing. Ten things or behaviours you are really happy, excited, proud, or grateful about being or having in your life right now. And say thank you! Really feel it and say it out loud. For each one of them. Say thanks three times for good measure.

That's where it starts. Inside of you. It's never about others or the things we want. Start right now – being who you want to be. It will amaze you how your perspective on life changes. And you end up with the way of life you REALLY want. Not because of the things you get or how others around you react. But because of who you have become.

There is a coaching model called be-do-have. It turns our perspective upside down (or front to back to be correct), as we normally go in the opposite order: I want to have x, so I must do y, then I will be z (insert emotion here). Much easier to start with the being.

Hip, hip, hoooooorrraayyyyyyy for BEING.

★ **Reflections?**

★ **One action I'll take**

Follow yourself.

Follow yourself. So many things to do. So many people to do things for. So many books to read, podcasts to listen to. We get lost in the "world out there", all the external things we want and have to do and must keep up with.

What if I said that the biggest journey to be had is the internal one? Of following yourself. Of finding your way back to that inner compass – in case you've lost track. As leaders, business owners, parents and influencers of the communities we're part of, it's easy to get so focused on the task at hand that we lose track of ourselves for a moment.

To be there for ourselves, to accept ALL that we are – including all the stuff we're not proud of, the traits we want to hide, the quirks so different to those of everybody else. Shame loves shadows. The thing we're embarrassed about? Hiding it makes it grow. Hiding it makes it spiral.

We are strong as leaders and human beings when we have nothing to hide. When we can accept others for what they are – not letting their different ways of being and doing things push our buttons.

So, what about making it an inner journey? To (re)find that path that supports YOU, getting back to what you do really well, what lights you up. The little joys and passions we've forgotten. And it doesn't mean shedding everything else in your life – all the external things can stay exactly as they are. You are moulding yourself in new ways and shifting on the inside, carving out little ten-minute pockets to nurture YOU, getting back the spark in your eyes — not changing the world, but adjusting how you experience the world around you.

Following yourself is not a selfish thing to do. It's the only thing to do. Because we're all different. Nobody is exactly like you. So how could their path or view be exactly right for you? We get inspiration from each other. We can find role models to copy. We can grow by sharing our experiences and views with others and by taking on their feedback. But only you can shine your light. So, stay true to your compass. Follow yourself.

★ **Reflections?**

★ **One action I'll take**

When a lot is not enough ...

On Danish TV, there is a show called *De Perfekte Piger* (The Perfect Girls), where four girls in their early twenties meet weekly to help each other let go of the mask of the perfect girl. Can you think of any other country that would produce a show like that? Well, I don't know any other countries I've lived or worked in that would.

It's pretty confronting to watch because it's not glamorous or a talk show or famous people surviving on an island; it's everyday girls. And it's confronting because most of you reading this will either know the perfect girl because she is you or have girls or women in your lives who fill that role all too well … They may be 8, 11, 14, 17, 21, 35, 47, 56, 69, 77, 84, or … They try so hard, and it's never enough.

The issue is that when we define perfect in our heads, it's based on the best possible façade that we see others put on during school, work, family gatherings, shopping, or on social media. It is based on the little pockets in time when someone, somewhere has got it all together. It's NEVER a realistic full-week-in-someone's-life where you compare your everyday life to their everyday life, with all the ups and downs, disappointments and joys, misunderstandings and glimpses of contentment.

It's a comparison that will never be to your advantage.

So, you may have kept it together, being the good girl (aiming at perfect) at school, in your work, maybe even creating a family and having a go at making that perfect as well (how crazy is that: adding two-plus more people and potential pets into the mix and still pretending spotless is possible??).

The only way out is realising that it's not possible. That you need to open up to people you know and trust and share the things that are not ideal. Having places and moments in which it's OK to take off the mask and be YOU. With your vulnerability, your fears, your doubts, your inner critic. Realising that the more YOU dare to show the full side of you, the more you allow others to be themselves too.

So, what about making this coming week a matter-of-fact one? Not pretending to have it all together, but taking it all as it comes, being realistic and accepting that not everything has to be glossy and pretty. Look for someone to open up to, so you don't bottle it all up. Look to find friends in your life you can have a good cry and a laugh with, sharing all the disappointments – of ourselves, our partners, our jobs, our kids, our families, our neighbours …

We need to realise we DO have a choice. That it's often ourselves who create this idea that we have to do it all ourselves, and do it perfectly. That's a lot of pressure to put on ourselves.

And realise that it's never too late. The girls on the program are in their early twenties — but even if you're in the late double digits, why not have a go at shaking her off, the perfect girl? If you did shake her off, what could life look like instead?

★ **Reflections?**

★ **One action I'll take**

Two years from now – who are you?

Two years from now, what are you doing? Who are you being? This is not a career question, as you may first think.

I look back and see so many wonderful changes. Because I made a decision nearly two years ago out of pure passion and feeling it was right.

What is one little thing that you will start doing for pure joy? Because you would love to. Because doing that thing, say once a month, will make you happy and allow you to start connecting again with how joy feels. Not because someone thinks you should do it, or they think it would be great for you – but because YOU have a yearning to give it a go.

Make that decision now! It can be something tiny. It can be a new hobby. Or an hour doing absolutely nothing, purposely. You only need to carve out one hour for YOU, say once a month, to explore and do this thing.

Now imagine two years from now. How much joy and energy has that activity or non-activity given you? And what are the ripple effects in other areas of your life and on the people in your life??!! What are you waiting for?

I'm heading out to find a hula hoop to play with. Haven't done that since I was a kid. And not for a purpose. Just for fun. And who knows? Now that I have made up my mind, I may come across one in the street, put out for a council collection. See you soon!

★ **Reflections?**

★ **One action I'll take**

Like teenagers again.

Some friends of ours slept in the car the other week. After a great night, they'd come back to where they'd left the kids, at the grandparents' place, and found themselves locked out. It can't get more teenager than that – sleeping the last few hours of the night in a car outside your parents' place. Fabulous.

That's exactly what we need to do more of. All of us. Enjoying ourselves, taking time to just be, having fun with people we like hanging out with. Exactly like we (may or may not!) have done as teenagers. If you didn't, grab a second chance. We have been celebrating lots of friends' fiftieth birthdays lately, and many of us have that freedom returning as the kids start to look after themselves.

But it doesn't matter if you have kids or not. If you're in your 20s, 30s, or 40s. In a high-pressure career or retired – it doesn't matter at all. The point is, as we're so busy becoming responsible adults, doing the things we've seen others do as adults, we forget. We forget that the most important thing is to keep your childlike curiosity alive, to tap into your teenage-like enjoyment and be laissez-faire now and then.

What's something teenage-ish you can do today? An hour of "I don't care about rules and responsibilities", whether it's having a beer on the balcony in your undies, crashing in front of your favourite TV show with a big tub of ice cream, losing yourself in a book in your PJs and not bothering to have a shower, swapping (used) chewing gum with your partner, spending hours experimenting what sounds you can get out of an empty bottle, dropping in uninvited to a friend's, sleeping on the beach — whatever. A bit gross, a bit stupid, a bit embarrassing. Do it!

Take the best of the teenage years and add little doses into everyday life — leaving out the tormenting, painful parts that are best left behind. How good is that?

It's a good thing, taking on responsibility, and good on us all for spending hours keeping the world going around. But we end up being SO serious, putting so much pressure on ourselves and others. What if it didn't matter, just for a bit? I'm giggling already, thinking of the odd things you'll all be adventuring into this week … Have fun!!

★ **Reflections?**

★ **One action I'll take**

Deepen your connections

Including a few stories about me and nature

No pets allowed — well, maybe a bunny if you force me.

Growing up I never had a pet to call my own. My brother had a budgie and a lovely dog that became our family friend, but I never went close to the birdcage and really hated how his room smelled of old cucumber. I did walk the dog now and then (my brother paid me to do so!) and did confess a few sad feelings to it. But there was no big connection.

So when our kids started asking for pets, it was a clear NO. They're messy and need feeding and cleaning. And I would freak out if anyone put a bird near me – and pretend to be a statue if someone's dear cat got close to me on the couch. After long discussions, we agreed on two goldfish in a bowl. The kids lost interest after a while – one died, and we donated the other to the school's collection.

We did try having a dog for a week. A rescue dog that we checked out carefully, but as it started to settle in to the new surroundings of our home, its issues came out in full force, with bared teeth, biting, and compulsive behaviour. So we decided to take him back.

But here I am, mid-life, silently thanking my children for introducing first a bunny and then a budgie into our family. They brought something out in me that had been hidden, deeeeeeeeep down. Someone to care for, to talk to, to give a pat. OK, here I can hear my kids shouting: "But you have us!!!!"

I do, and I love you to bits, kids, but it's kind of harder to be a parent than a pet owner. So sitting with a pet on your lap is 1.0 Caring – keeping it very simple.

So … don't do it for your kids only. And choose a bunny or budgie as the first leap into this world. It's a bit hard connecting with a goldfish and anything bigger will work against time for YOUR passions (we don't need to say which blog number to go back to, right?). Happy hopping.

★ **Reflections?**

★ **One action I'll take**

**Nature?
No, thanks.
I tend to kill any
plants within a
20-metre radius.**

I'm a city girl. I had no idea what the stuff in the supermarket looked like originally (vacuum-packed slices of ham … no real connection to a live animal. And frozen vegetables … no idea how they would look in nature and if they grew on bushes or in the ground). I did go to a farm with school once and wrote a nice essay about it. But I had no idea or interest in the missing link.

I did have a phase with cacti (on my windowsill) because they could survive even if I didn't look their way for weeks. And I did like it when our family got peas out of some square metres of a garden patch one year.

A friend once asked me to look after her plants. Bad move. Overwatered most of them and really had no clue what I was doing. Nearly as bad a move as when I became an au pair after only having looked after one kid for one night. Amazing what people trust you with, just because you look kind of normal and sound sensible. A school girlfriend did give me a book with easy steps to follow to look after the most popular pot plants, and I did manage to keep a succulent alive for some months. Once.

But here's the amazing thing: I've come to treasure nature. I've managed to keep some plants alive for several years now (including performing some resurrections). And I've started being interested in buying food that is as close to its natural state as possible.

Even if I still don't have a green thumb, I feel connected with nature and actually do have a chat with some trees and wild animals from time to time. (Sorry, kids. I embarrassed you again, didn't I?) So even if I can't do magic with nature's crops yet, at least we spend some time together.

Happy gardening this weekend (or just sitting on a bench watching a flower!) – treasure your skills, however minimal.

★ **Reflections?**

★ **One action I'll take**

Young girls out there — listen to that inner voice!

Listen to your inner voice. When things go wrong for you, when you get a dent in your car, drop things, or hurt your finger, it's a gentle nod to you that you're not listening to that inner voice. That you have been caught up in thoughts or actions that are draining you more than giving you energy. That it's time to stop and listen.

Do something good for yourself, something that grounds you. Go for a walk in nature, be silent (NO, Insta or Snapchat friends do NOT need to know; this one is for YOU). Just be open to what messages your inner voice is trying to send – you have powered through without listening, so it needs to "trip you up" in bigger and bigger ways and shout at you, as long as you're still not listening.

Meditation sounds like such a Hare Krishna thing, I know. I only tried it out last year – and it's not that dangerous!! It really just forces you to be absolutely still. What is that inner voice telling you? Are you chasing fame and others' approval, when really you could be doing all the same things you are doing but in a way right for you? Be grounded, and be the best YOU that you can manage today.

Here's a great metaphor that I was told once: "Look after your own garden." Imagine a garden with a little fence around it. What will YOU grow? Maybe only grass to keep it easy. Or some nice flowers. Imagine their colours and fragrance. Now here comes your best friend, who pops their head over the fence with some potatoes from THEIR garden that they think you should grow as well. Do you see the point?

Maybe you say yes and become a lover of growing potatoes, but it's OK to say "no, thanks" – and wait for whatever idea you get next about what you want to grow. You don't have to live your life in a way that conforms to others' demands. Others will try to get you to do things they think are right. Regardless of whether their intentions are good or bad, what's right in their world may not be right in yours.

You can do exactly the same tasks and things that you do now – but do them for you, be true to you! Maybe you will do them with your current friends. Maybe over time, you'll start noticing who it's easy to be yourself around – and spend more time with them.

So, start looking for the small trip-ups in daily life and THANK your inner voice for that reminder.

★ **Reflections?**

★ **One action I'll take**

Meditation — HA! I bet my brain will never be able to stop racing.

Breathe in. Breathe out.

Again.

It took me half a lifetime to realise it's good to stop … I hope others will realise it much earlier. Imagine how much resistance that would save your friends and family – and you!

My first attempt at stopping for a moment was through Pilates. Strengthening my core to keep my lower back issues at bay. A great thing to do while you brush your teeth or wait in a supermarket queue – a win-win because you'll be happy when your queue turns out to be the slowest one. I did bring my (three-year-old) daughter with me. "SO boring" she said. No surprise really, as a Pilates class looks like people lying on the floor for a full hour doing nothing. You can't see all the inner work going on.

I digress. In my twenties, I never looked back, inwards, or anywhere other than full speed ahead. In an all-time-low year (relationship and job ended, on my own in a new city, lonely as, just had my wisdom teeth out – the irony!), I went to a palm reader. Wise woman. She commented on me being a perfectionist (?!), and said that I would have a partner move out of the bedroom before my fortieth if I didn't let go of that perfectionism! At that point, I did not even have a boyfriend. I was probably such a powerful young woman that most boys didn't even dare look my way. But, boy, did she have a point! A strong suggestion to stop and smell the roses.

Breathe in. Breathe out.

Luckily, I tried meditation. Another attempt at stopping for a moment. It's not at all scary! My busy mind is having SO much fun. Some days, I visualise running in the bush or swimming across a pool — and have not moved a muscle! And thoughts come and go, and you can just imagine hanging them with pegs on a clothesline as you go along your way. How easy is that?

So do yourself a favour. Stop now and then and smell those roses.

Breathe in. Breathe out.

Aaaaaaaaah …

★ **Reflections?**

★ **One action I'll take**

Say yes and work out how

It's all nothing without action

51

Me – masculine??!!! That wasn't the goal ...

What's YOUR percentage split of masculine versus feminine energy? Because we DO have both. John Gray did the world a lot of good with his *Men Are from Mars, Women Are from Venus*. It does explain a LOT around how to understand each other better and live together in a more fruitful way. So, if you haven't already, read it. Just like anyone working or living with Greeks should watch *My Big Fat Greek Wedding* … Anyway … sidetrack.

When we go to the next level and see behind our "labels", there is a delicate balance of masculine AND feminine energies in us all; no energy is confined to one gender. It is very helpful to know your dominant energy – and be aware of where you have some learning to do still. The good old idea of opposite forces working in tandem.

The more you can use BOTH sides of the energy within yourself, the more balanced you will be, the more success you will find, and the more positive results you will create with ALL types of humans (probably animals as well – who knows?!).

For many years, I treasured my drive, my freedom, my ability to let go, my independence, my power, and all the other typical masculine energy qualities. I preferred hanging out with and talking to men (and all my female friends were strong as …). When I became a mother, I realised that I couldn't deny it forever. There was something going on around the power of the feminine energies – the more inferential communication, the gathering, the caring, the cyclical ways of creating results, the vulnerability and sensitivity.

This "quest for my feminine side" has been going on for almost sixteen years now, with SO much learning and laughter coming from getting to know our two awesome daughters and the amazing number of influential women that I have met and treasure.

 AUTHOR'S NOTE: Ooops how time flies. I've had another seven years to practise since I wrote this, with the oldest now 23. From the trenches: it works!

A lot of these women have STACKS of masculine energy, but the real treasures pop up when we allow the other side, the vulnerability and the space we give others, to be added to the mix.

And now a purposeful sidetrack: how masculine is goal setting, the way we're used to doing it? Masculine energy works best with one clear goal, with a specific start and finish date, that requires you to work towards it with a tunnel focus. Does this sound like the way typical corporate goals operate, hmm?

Feminine energy, on the other hand, is more process-driven and delivers best through three to six goals you work on at the same time in a cyclical way. "Over summer, I will get a healthy food regime set up/ write my book." Of course, when working towards several goals at once, you need to be realistic with the timelines (six concurrent projects NEED a longer timeline than one focused project). And it's helpful to put more energy into the one closest to your heart. How interesting is this? I'm definitely feminine in this sense, so it's been a true revelation.

So how engaged do you feel with the goals you or others set for you? Have a go at defining them in a different way and see what happens!

And linking back to your natural energy balance – is it about time YOU get some more masculine energy going? Or for some of you, is it time to nurture activities that allow the feminine to have a word for once? Enjoy fine-tuning your balance.

★ **Reflections?**

★ **One action I'll take**

GOODBYE SUPERWOMAN

One year for women – or one day?

Years ago, I shared the following article, and I'm humbled by the progress I continue to witness from people in my circles, to promote more women to do what they do best. So, let's make it an everyday intention, not just a focus once a year?

International Women's Day. I treasure women. I treasure men. I don't think we need special days – just like we don't make a big deal of "Father's Day" and "Mother's Day" in our house. I respect and admire all the strong and brave people who made it possible for us to live with the rights we have today. And I acknowledge many people need better lives still.

But last year, US women were encouraged to not work and not spend on this day, to show how society's wheels would not turn without us. And in Australia, some companies have started ratios for how many women you need to hire. I don't think that's the way.

Progress is created not by opposition, provocation, or rules, but by visionary humans (men and women). Respecting each other, finding the root cause when things are not right yet, and then encouraging each other to take the brave steps needed.

We all have both masculine and feminine energy and drive. Using both creates a formidable force – and those heroes we celebrate today, and every day, would have used a finely tuned combination of both.

So, let's be the best version of ourselves. On as many days as possible. Celebrating our diversity and the magic that happens when we combine our strengths. Every day.

★ **Reflections?**

★ **One action I'll take**

Keep turning up!

AUTHOR'S NOTE: YES, this is the 53th blog, the added bonus, the complimentary addition not fitting the 52-blog title. Even if your perfectionist tics may have started (she can't call it 52 blogs and include 53!), this blog may be the most important one of them all, so stay with me!

When you feel like quitting. When it all gets too hard. When others think you shouldn't keep going. DON'T quit. Instead, keep turning up.

It's not always the smartest, luckiest, or richest who end up being the happy ones, the ones living the life they truly want. It can be. But the most important point is we ALL can be that person. And the thing that makes the biggest difference is whether you keep turning up.

A helpful question from John Assaraf (known to some of you from *The Secret*) is: "Are you interested, or are you committed?" This distinction is crucial to achieving your goals and dreams.

What is that "thing" you're working on at the moment? Is it creating a loving, kind family while being the best human being you can possibly be? Is it finishing the study you've been doing for a while? Is it getting that room cleaned up? Is it starting to look after yourself and your health by exercising? Fill in YOUR focus.

Now answer this. Are you interested or are you committed to achieving this?

If you're interested, you'll only do what's convenient. And you'll let the excuses hold you back. If you're committed, you will do whatever it takes to overcome any setbacks, issues, and events around you. Because they WILL pop up. It won't just be smooth sailing. Others may not agree with how you choose to spend your time and focus.

So, when you have something that's important to you, keep going. Keep turning up. Keep taking little steps all the time to become the person you want to become, the person you need to be to achieve it. The person your future self will thank you for becoming.

Sometimes success is NOT getting what you want. What matters is how you deal with it. Deal with all the stuff that life sends your way. Be aware of how it triggers your emotions and respond with grace. And keep turning up. Feeling that you've made the effort, had a go. Taken one step towards that goal.

What does it look like, sound like, and feel like when you keep turning up, despite the circumstances? Keep turning up. You've got this!

★ **Reflections?**

★ **One action I'll take**

Acknowledgements

Thank you. Thank you for your time. Thank you for buying, borrowing or stealing this book. Thanks for reading my stories. From my heart, I hope parts of it have made sense, and that some nuggets of gold have been passed from me to you.

I'm grateful for all the teachers in my life. This is a broad definition of my family, friends, colleagues, role models, nature, animals, and experiences traditionally labelled good or bad. Thanks for making this daily journey of learning so thrilling. Thank you Remi Sharon Pearson and team TCI (The Coaching Institute) for igniting my fire when I was ready.

I feel very humbled to have been a teacher myself for thousands of people through my years of full-time coaching, writing, and running workshops. Covering a wide range of topics from basic life hacks to mindset and human behaviour, communication, business strategy, sales, and leadership.

Applying an (often annoying?) laser-sharp finger on the root cause and helping create solutions. Allowing you to bring all your superpowers into play. We are so clever that we often let our minds run the show, whereas the positive reach and the implications are far superior when we combine all our superpowers: not just our head but heart, gut and maybe a little toe – who knows where that intuition and inner wisdom reside. A big part of coaching is letting go of what the 'world' thinks we should do, and get curious about our own suggestions.

Thank you to all of those I've connected with over the years for letting me into your world. For letting me help connect the dots and create clarity. For letting me show you that you're exactly as you're supposed to be; there is nothing that needs fixing. Instead of fixing, it's about accepting ourselves with all our quirks. (Then adding skills to create the everyday life and outcomes we really want.)

I wish you all the best. Dig deep for your truth and your full potential. The world needs you – just the way you are.

Tak, tak, tak. That's thanks in Danish. Three of them for good measure.

About the Author

My name is Annlone Dalhoff, and I'm a musician, mother and lover of nature. I'm also a multilingual corporate strategist and marketing director, with decades of experience in global and local businesses, and years ago I trained to become a mindset coach and business coach.

Originally from Denmark, I came to Australia with my family in 2008. Drawn here by the opportunity to take on a senior executive role in a global business, but also driven by curiosity, a sense of adventure and the desire to learn and grow as a family in a new culture.

We're still here, and over time we've all grown. In fact it's that desire to grow, to push ourselves a little bit further that I truly enjoy, and that's what prompted me to train as a coach to help more people bring everything they've got to the party.

I used to be a big-time perfectionist, bossy boss and high achiever. Ten years ago, I started a journey of allowing myself to be vulnerable. To just BE. To listen and be present more than being busy fixing. I'm so grateful for all the brave work I put in. That I dared to let go of perfectionism and over-achieving in every single aspect of my life and work. I still am both, but today I choose when to apply them and when not. What a gift. For me and everybody around me.

90 different words describe me now according to my network, and ChatGPT sorted them into the following buckets: Leadership, Energy, Happiness, Curiosity and Friendliness. It struggled to label Fårehyrde (shepherd) and Cheefunker (funny, cheeky, clever). Anyway, the journey of shedding those Bossy Pants takes bravery but is highly recommended.

I'm sharing the 52 Sunday blogs to inspire you to live life to your own tune. Extracts from 8 years of 'A Kick or a Carrot' blogging as part of my journey finding my feet as a woman, a mother, a wife and a leader while becoming a certified Mindset coach and starting my Joy Hearts Coaching business – later Dalhoff Consulting focusing on Leadership, Mindset, Business and Sales coaching. Thanks for reading.

What people say about Annlone

Annlone has a unique ability to grasp the core issues, challenge held "beliefs" and get teams to focus on the matter at hand.
Karen de Leeuw, Sydney

Bad-ass & fun.
Michael Taylor, CEO Lionize

An hour with Annlone is like a week on an island. You come out refreshed, orientated and clear.
Nick Wormald, Managing Director Grow Capital

An extraordinary energy and a laser-sharp focus.
Nikola Ellis, Director, Adore Yoga

What's Next

If you've read the book (there's no assuming here – I know plenty of people who jump straight to the end!) but didn't capture your reflections and one action after each blog, go back and have another read.

Moving things from our head to paper makes a crucial difference. We did not create a workbook, so if you don't want to write in your nice book or are listening to the audiobook version, this is a great excuse to buy yourself a new, colourful notebook on the side. Capturing your thoughts in writing will make a difference to your intentions and outcomes. I'm telling you!

If you're the classical curious student who wants to invest more into your journey, hire a coach or start with the Goodbye Superwoman reading list on the joyhearts.com.au website.

Being curious and brave will take you far, inside and out. Feel free to connect as well or follow me on the socials. I can't help myself, always sharing random kicks and carrots, and hope it will continue to stir reflection and spark action. See you.

- facebook.com/annlone.dalhoff
- instagram.com/annlone_d/
- linkedin.com/in/annlone-dalhoff/
- joyhearts.com.au
- dalhoffconsulting.com

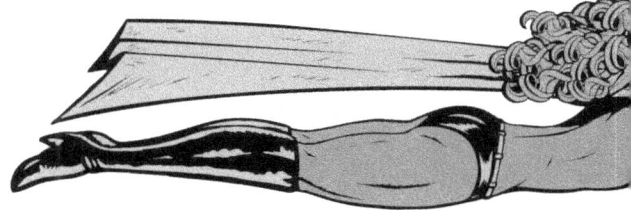

www.ingramcontent.com/pod-product-compliance
Lightning Source LLC
Chambersburg PA
CBHW042344300426
44109CB00050B/2866